the very

# the internet

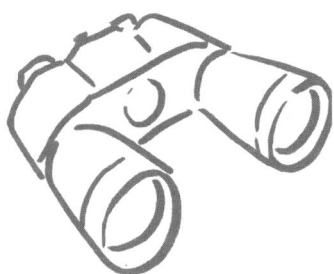

Zingin.com

Prentice
Hall

An Imprint of Pearson Education

London New York Toronto Sydney Tokyo
Singapore Madrid Mexico City Munich Paris

PEARSON EDUCATION LIMITED

*Head Office:*
Edinburgh Gate
Harlow
Essex CM20 2JE
Tel: +44 (0)1279 623623
Fax: +44 (0)1279 431059

*London Office:*
128 Long Acre
London WC2E 9AN
Tel: +44 (0)20 7447 2000
Fax: +44 (0)20 7240 5771

First published in Great Britain in 2000

ISBN 0-130-40938-3

The right of Paul Carr to be identified as author of
this work has been asserted by it in accordance with the
Copyright, Designs and Patents Act 1988.

*British Library Cataloguing-in-Publication Data*
A catalogue record for this book can be obtained from the British Library.

Many of the designations used by manufacturers and sellers to
distinguish their products are claimed as trademarks. Pearson Education
Limited has made every attempt to supply trademark information about
manufacturers and their products mentioned in this book.

10  9  8  7  6  5  4  3  2  1

Typeset by Land & Unwin (Data Sciences) Ltd
Printed and bound by Ashford Colour Press, Gosport, Hampshire

*The publishers' policy is to use paper manufactured from sustainable forests.*

# contents

# introduction

Finding what you're looking for on the internet can be like trying to find a very small needle in a very large haystack.

There are billions of pages on millions of sites, and somewhere in the middle of it all is the information you need. The difficult part is knowing where to look.

When we originally launched Zingin.com the plan was to create a site which would make it easier for UK internet users to get straight to the best of the web. Although both the site and the internet itself have grown massively since those early days, we're still dedicated to helping make sense out of the chaos – which is where this book comes in.

So who's it written for? Well, if you're a UK internet user who wants to search the web more effectively then it's for you. No matter whether you're searching for information about music, 18th-century French architecture or a decent recipe for macaroni cheese, we're here to point you towards the best directories, search engines and guides for the job.

We've tried to make it as easy as possible for you to just dive in and get started with the book. The chapters have been put in a (hopefully) logical order, starting with sites which help you to find general UK and global information, then those which specialise in searching for particular types of site – and finally all of the other useful search tools including people finders, discussion groups and even mobile sites for WAP users.

Although only the very best of the web has made it into these pages, each section is headed by a site which we call **the best of the best** so you don't have to waste any time getting started, and, if you know the name of the site you want, you can look it up in the quick reference section tucked away neatly at the back.

With the help of this book it should be pretty straight-forward to find the information you're looking for, but if you do have any problems please come and visit us on the web (**www.zingin.com**) and we'll try our best to help you out.

Happy searching!

*Paul Carr*
*Founder*
*Zingin.com*

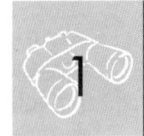

# the internet:
# a (very) brief guide

The fact that you've bought this book means that you've probably used the internet before, either at home or at work. If, however, you're still getting to grips with the basics then read on for the answers to some of our most frequently asked questions.

## Getting started

There are plenty of online resources to help you get the most out of the web, but they're no use if you're not online. By far the quickest way to get started is to pop into your local newsagent or computer shop and get hold of one of the many free internet access CDs stuck to the front of popular computer magazines. However, if you want a bit more information before taking the plunge, have a quick look at the following pointers.

### I'm new to the internet: how do I get started?

It goes without saying that to take advantage of the information contained in this book, you'll need access to the internet. If you want to connect from home you'll need a computer (a 486 or above should be fine), a modem (new computers usually come with one built in) and a spare telephone socket within easy reach of the computer.

The modem, which plugs in to the back of your computer (unless it's already built in) and then into the telephone socket, has basically one purpose – to allow your computer to send and receive data over a telephone line. Once you're plugged in, all that remains now is to decide which internet service provider (ISP) you will use to get connected. Your ISP provides a gateway to the internet and when you ask your computer to connect to the web or to send and receive emails, your modem is actually dialling into their network which, in turn, is connected to the rest of the internet. This explains how you can send an email to Egypt or to Edinburgh for the same price – you're only paying for the call to the ISP (the price of a local call or less). If you don't want to connect from home then most large libraries provide free or low-cost internet access and there are plenty of internet cafés around the UK which will be happy to help you take your first online steps.

## Which ISP is right for me?

Choosing an ISP can be a complicated business, with some companies giving free access, some offering free telephone calls and a few still clinging on to monthly charges – all trying to persuade you that you'll get a better deal with them. Pretty confusing. Basically, the right ISP for you will depend on what you want to use the internet for.

If you're only interested in email, surfing the web and maybe building a personal website, then you'll be fine with a free service. Of course, there's no such thing as a free lunch and you'll usually still have to pay either local call charges or a fixed fee for unlimited access. Luckily for internet users, there's fierce competition among ISPs and you can find some excellent deals if you shop around. To get online with a free service you can either pick up a connection CD from one of the high street shops which have set up their own ISPs (WHSmith, PC World, Waterstone's and Tesco, to name just a few) or call up one of the providers advertised in any of the popular internet magazines.

If you want to use the internet for business and require extra features such as high-speed access, a business website or your own domain name (e.g. **www.yourname.com**) then you'll need to use a specialist ISP which will usually charge a monthly fee in addition to your normal phone charges.

If you already have internet access at work, university,

school or in a local internet café then surf over to ISP Review (www.ispreview.co.uk) for a full rundown of the best and worst UK internet service providers.

## Online help and advice

OK, so you've made it online and you're looking for help and advice on how to get the most out of the web. Of course, to find the best websites to get you started you'll want to take a quick trip to your friends at

Zingin.com (www.zingin.com) but for technical support and general advice, try the following.

## Why does it say that the page I'm looking for is not found?

The internet is in a constant state of development and things are getting moved around and deleted all the time. Anyone who's spent more than a couple of minutes on the web will have clicked on a link or typed in a web address only to get hit with the dreaded 'File not found' message. If the page you're looking for seems to have vanished, the most likely cause is that the page has been deleted or moved to another address. If an address doesn't work, try removing bits from the end until you find something.

For example, if the address www.asite.com/directory/files/filename.html produces an error, try deleting the 'filename.html' bit to see if there's anything at www.asite.com/directory/files. If you're still getting an error then try www.asite.com/directory and finally www.asite.com. If you run out of things to delete and still can't find the site then it's probably temporarily unavailable or has been deleted. Sites that have been moved can often be tracked down using a search engine such as Google (www.google.com) – simply type in the name of the page/site and see what comes up.

## What is the best software for browsing the web?

Most of the free ISPs include a copy of Microsoft Internet Explorer on their access CDs and, unless you really want to, there's no real need to use another browser. If you do fancy a change or want to fight back against Microsoft's quest for world domination, there are some alternatives worth trying.

The best of the bunch is Netscape Navigator, which contains a very similar range of features to Internet Explorer but with slightly less polish. Comparing Netscape and Internet Explorer is a bit like comparing Burger King and McDonald's – try them both and decide which one tastes better. Other choices can be found at **www.browserwatch.com**.

## How can I find out more about using the web?

The internet used to be controlled by academics, scientists and computer geeks, and unless you knew your way around it could be very scary indeed. In cyberspace no one could hear you scream.

Nowadays, using email and surfing the web is like driving a car – pretty straightforward when you get the hang of it, even if you don't know exactly what's going on under the bonnet. Having said that, if you want to get the most out of your internet experience you'll need to get a basic grasp of the way it works. One of the best guides to how the net works and what it can do is Learn the Net (**www.learnthenet.com**), which contains some very well-written tutorials covering e-mail, downloading files, building a website and plenty of other useful stuff. If you're baffled by internet jargon you'll definitely want to have a quick look at PC Webopedia (**www.pcwebopedia.com**) and, for advice with a UK perspective visit BBC Webwise (**www.bbc.co.uk/webwise**).

## How can I stop my children finding unsuitable material on the web?

One of the main concerns about the growth of the internet is the ease with which children can find unsuitable material online. Due to the global and unrestricted nature of the web, it is very easy to find material with an adult theme – some of it illegal under UK law. In order to keep your family safe on the web, there are a number of steps you can take.

● **Install family filter software**
  Companies such as Net Nanny (**www.netnanny.com**) and Cyber Patrol (**www.cyberpatrol.com**) offer software which runs in the background on your computer, restricting access to unsuitable material. However, no software is foolproof and children should always be supervised when surfing the internet.

● **Don't allow unrestricted use of search engines**
  Teaching children to use search engines can improve their computer literacy but also provides quick and

easy access to the worst of the web – even the most innocent of searches can return adult results. If children are to be given access to search engines, look for one with a family filter built in which screens out unsuitable results. For UK searches try UK Plus (www.ukplus.com) and, for searching the whole web, use the family filter option on AltaVista (www.altavista.com).

- **Chat rooms and email**
  Children often enjoy using the internet to keep in touch with friends through chat rooms or via email. Always take the same precautions with this type of communication as you would with other internet use. The danger of talking to strangers is just as real on the internet as in the real world!

- **Supervise, supervise, supervise**
  As well as being a great way to spend quality time with your family, supervising children while they use the internet is vital to avoid them accessing adult content. For older children, it is often wise to remove the telephone cable from your modem if you are going out and leaving them in the house! As in the real world, however, there are some very real dangers online which can be avoided by simply monitoring your family's internet use.

## Buying online

Throughout this book you'll find sites that allow you to order products, book tickets and generally spend your hard-earned cash. The first thing to remember is that using your credit card online is 100% safe providing you take a few sensible precautions.

## How do I know which companies to trust?

Firstly, wherever possible stick to companies you've heard of. If someone you know has bought from a particular site without any problems or if it's a household name then the risk is greatly reduced.

As with any purchase on or off the web, you should always ensure that you are buying from a reputable company. Sites such as Amazon (www.amazon.co.uk) and Lastminute.com (www.lastminute.com) are very well-known internet traders and so are a risk-free option, but if you do want to order from a company you've never heard of then take a look at the next few questions which will hope-fully address your concerns.

## Can hackers get hold of my credit card number once I've typed it in?

As long as you only type your credit card details into sites that offer encryption security (SSL), your information will be perfectly safe. Look for a yellow padlock on the bottom right of your browser window if you are using Internet Explorer; in Netscape look for a closed padlock. This ensures that information sent to the site is encrypted and so cannot be intercepted by hackers. If the site is not secure, be very wary about placing an online order and never *ever* send credit card information via normal email.

## How can I check on the status of my order?

Many larger sites offer order tracking facilities which allow you to check the progress of your order until it is delivered. If there is no order tracking, ensure there is a contact telephone number in case you need to chase things up.

## Is it safe to order from outside the UK?

Orders placed with companies outside the UK are not protected by UK sale of goods or safety legislation. Only order from abroad if you know and trust the company you are dealing with; even then, try to stick within Western Europe and the USA.

## Am I going to get stung by hidden costs?

There's no 'internet tax' for orders made online but, as with any mail order purchase, you should always check whether your order includes postage and packing costs. Also, remember that orders from outside the UK may be subject to additional customs and import costs.

## Is there a regulatory body for online traders?

The Consumers' Association have been looking after the interests of shoppers for years and have recently launched a scheme to protect you on the web. The Which? Web Trader scheme (**www.which.net/webtrader**) requires its members to abide by a strict code of conduct if they want to join. Sites that have the Web Trader logo have to provide a decent level of service, otherwise Which? will simply kick them out! It's worth remembering that membership of the scheme isn't compulsory and many reputable businesses are not members, so if you don't see the logo don't assume the worst; but if you do, then expect the best.

## What if the goods don't arrive or my credit card is used fraudulently?

Don't panic if products ordered online take a while to arrive. Just like in the real world, delays do happen and things can be out of stock – even if you receive a confirmation saying that everything is fine. However, if you've waited longer than 21 days then you should contact the company concerned to hurry them up.

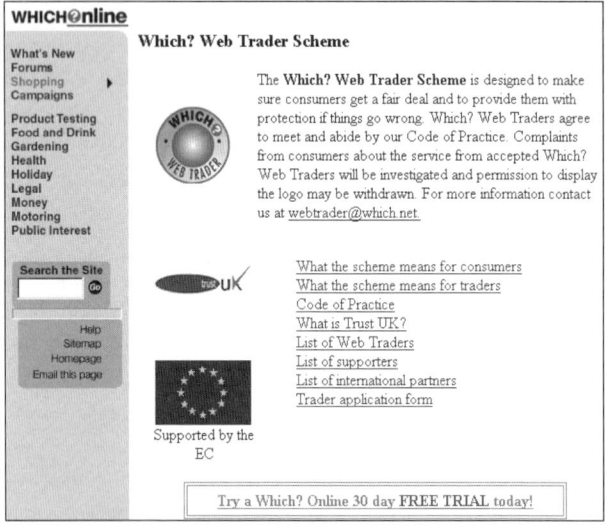

A gentle reminder will usually be enough to get things moving but if you're still not getting anywhere you should contact your credit card issuer for advice. If the site is a member of the Which? Web Trader scheme, make sure you let them know as well.

If you have problems with an order made using a credit card, you will usually be able to recover any lost money from your card issuer. If you're concerned about fraud, call your credit card company to check their policy regarding fraudulent transactions.

## Can I buy anything I like over the web?

Yes and no. Most things are available – from sweets and cakes to cars and houses. But you can't necessarily order them from the UK. The law on ordering from abroad using the internet is the same as using the phone, and there are certain products which it is illegal to bring into the country. Some good examples of this are: drugs, certain food items, adult material, pets and automatic weapons. You can probably guess the law's position on drugs and guns but if you need to check out what is allowed, visit Customs and Excise (www.hmce.gov.uk).

# 2

# top tips for stress-free searching

To search the internet you need a search tool. Using the right one – directory, search engine or metasearch tool – will help you locate what you're looking for without wasting time visiting hundreds of irrelevant sites. This subject is covered in more detail later, but here we offer a few tips to get you started.

Directories, search engines and metasearch tools all basically do the same job: they use keywords supplied by you to search the web for sites which may be of interest.

Keywords may be single words such as *Kendal, mint* and *cake*, or whole sentences like: '*Where can I find information about Kendal mint cake*'. Either way, the purpose is to get the best results from your chosen search tool.

## Know what makes them tick

Detailed knowledge of how a search tool works isn't necessary to use it but it may help to know a little about how your chosen method produces its results. We'll look at the three different search tools and explain briefly how each works.

A *search engine,* such as Google (**www.google.com**) or AltaVista (**www.altavista.co.uk**), is basically a huge database containing information about the location and contents of literally millions of web pages.

When you ask a search engine to find a site, rather than search the entire web (which would take too long to be practical), it uses keywords you have typed in and searches its database for pages where these words appear. These are then presented to you as a list of links with a brief description of where each one leads.

So, how can any search engine know about every page on the web?

The simple answer is – they can't. Even the biggest search engines like Google, which claims to be able to search over one billion sites, don't know everything, and given the rate at which the internet is expanding that's hardly surprising!

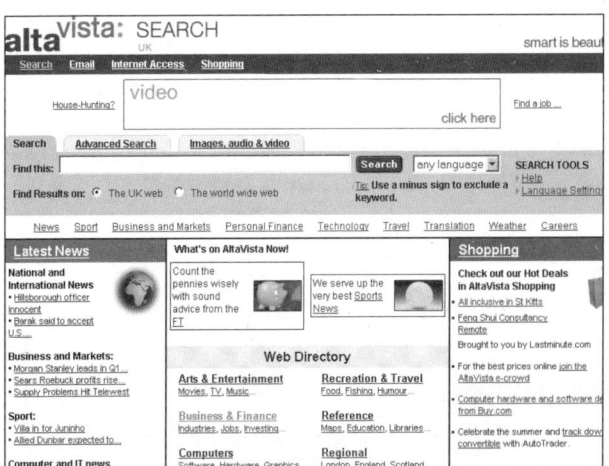

Having said that, there are so many search engines now that the information or page you are looking for will almost certainly be on one of them, so don't give up if your first search doesn't find what you're after.

Search engines discover new sites by using special software called 'spiders' or 'robots' which automatically bounce from one site to another recording information about the contents of each page, picking out the important keywords and storing it all in the database.

Next we consider *directories,* which work slightly differently. Instead of using robots to try to index every page on the web, they rely on real live human beings to choose the best sites. The style of directory sites varies considerably. Some, like Yahoo! (**www.yahoo.co.uk**), list millions of pages separated into thousands of different categories, whereas sites like About (**www.about.co.uk**) also list a huge number of pages but do so in a more structured and specialised way – try browsing through both types and you'll see what we mean.

Finally, there are *metasearch* sites which, rather than searching themselves, submit your keywords directly to the top search engines and directories, displaying the results on one page. For example, if you search for *Kendal mint cake* on a metasearch site like Dogpile (**www.dogpile.com**) you will get a summary of results from sources such as Yahoo!, Hotbot, AltaVista and Excite – very useful if you are looking for something specific and don't want to spend time trekking around the web.

## Remember, the clue's in the question

Despite the claims made for them, search tools are actually pretty dim-witted. If you type *spin doctors* into Yahoo! or

Google, they have no way of knowing whether your interest is in political advisers or pop groups. They simply look at the words you type in and try to match them with sites they know about.

So you need to think about the sort of words which are likely to appear on the type of page you're looking for. For example, on a site about political spin doctors you will probably find words like *politics*, *press* and *government* so it's a good idea to include these in your choice of keywords. If it's the band you're after, you might include *music*, *album* and *band*.

As a general rule, it's best to start with a small number of keywords – just enough to give an idea of what you are looking for. If you were doing the above search, you might want to type in something like *spin doctor politics* or, if you

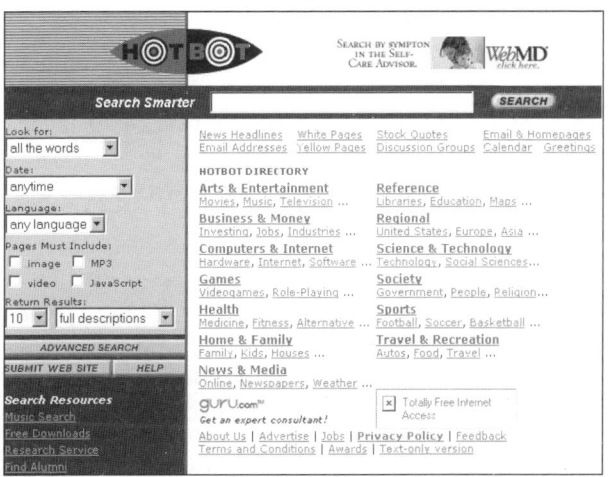

wanted to restrict your search to the UK, you might use *spin doctor politics UK*.

Having decided on your keywords, it's time to type them into the search box. There are a few tips which should help to produce better results. Firstly, unless you're specifically searching for something in upper case, like the AA or NASA, it's a good habit to use lower case for your keywords – *spin* and *SPIN* are completely different words to some search sites.

To find an exact phrase, e.g. *spin doctors* rather than merely those sites which happen to contain the words *spin* and *doctors*, enclose it in 'quotation marks'. A search for '*spin doctor*' would ignore pages about *spin* dryers and *Doctor* Spock.

Putting a plus sign in front of a keyword (*spin +doctor*) tells the search engine that doctor *must* be included (although the words can be in any order), while putting a minus sign (*spin –doctor*) means doctor *must not* be

included. This will help you either to focus your search or to avoid obvious but irrelevant links.

If you're feeling flash, some search engines invite you to use Boolean operators. These are basically the words *AND*, *OR* and *NOT*, which are put between keywords to produce more precise results. For example, a search for *spin AND doctors* would look for (you've guessed it) the words *spin* and *doctors*, while *spin NOT doctors* would exclude any page which contains the word *doctors*.

## Just browsing, thanks

An advantage with directories over search engines is that they are sorted into browsable categories. So, rather than using the search box, you can just click down through the subjects until you find what you need. As an example (and a shameless plug), if you look at the Zingin.com (**www.zin-gin.com**) front page you'll see a list of directory categories – Information, Family, Leisure, Shopping, etc. Clicking on, say, Leisure will take you to a list of sub-categories – Going Out, Film & Television, etc – each of which leads either to a list of recommended sites or, alternatively, another sub-category. Other examples of this type of structure can be found on Yahoo! and the Open Directory Project (**www.dmoz.org**).

## Ask a silly question – expect a silly answer

An increasing number of sites, such as Ask Jeeves (**www.ask.co.uk**), allow you to search using whole sentences rather than keywords (e.g. *where can I find ...*). Don't let these impress you too much – they still look at the main words in your question and use them to suggest possible matches so you still need to include as many keywords as possible. Asking *Where can I find information on spin doctors?* is just the same as typing in *spin doctors*. A much better question would be *Where can I find information on UK political spin doctors?*.

## Try a little Swiss Army searching

Search engines are always trying to keep up with the (virtual) Joneses when it comes to the range of features and tools they offer. Hotbot gave you the ability to search for pages which included music or video, so AltaVista

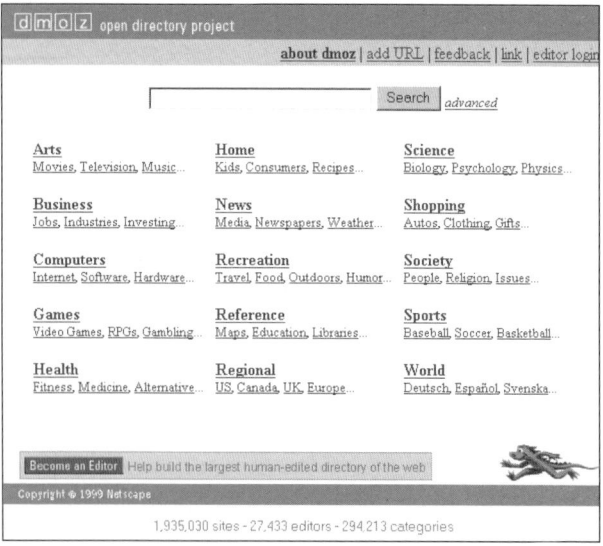

responded by allowing you to search for specific pictures. Not to be outdone, Google let you email the results to yourself (presumably in case you couldn't be bothered with reading them at the time), so Lycos countered with the ability to search for sites which hadn't even been built yet. OK, we made the last one up, but it can't be long until someone does. Some of the gimmicks and features are plain useless, but there are a few nifty ones which are covered in detail in the second half of this book.

## Never underestimate the power of guesswork

Sometimes, believe it or not, you don't need a search tool to find what you're looking for. If you are searching for the official site of a company such as Microsoft or Diesel then it's worth sticking *www.* at the start and *.com* (for international organisations) or *.co.uk* (for UK-based companies) on the end of the name and seeing where you end up. Diesel, for example, can be found at both **www.diesel.com** and **www.diesel.co.uk**, while Microsoft uses both **www.microsoft.com** and **www.microsoft.co.uk**. If you get the wrong site (or a 'page not found' error) then it might also be worth trying endings like *.org* (for organisations) and *.net* (for network providers).

## Get out there and try it!

Although the above tips are intended to make for simpler searching, by far the best way to learn is to choose a search engine and get stuck in. The worst that can happen is that you'll get some irrelevant results and, remember, every wrong keyword is another step on the road to search enlightenment. Choosing the right keywords is something of a knack which will come with practice, so do persevere – it'll pay dividends in the end. If you do get really stuck though, head over to the Zingin Search Guide (**www.zingin.com/ guide/search**) and we'll try our best to help you out.

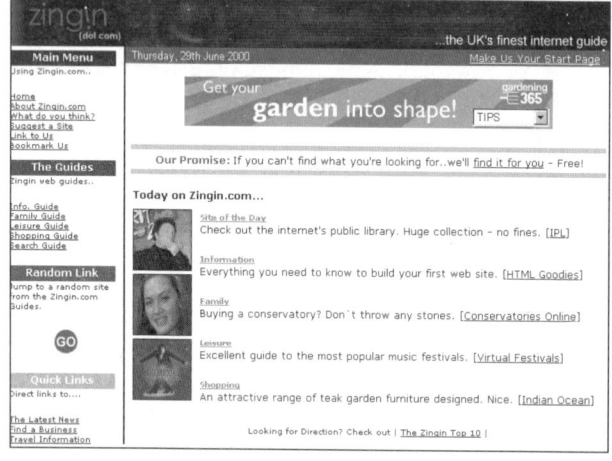

# general search tools

One of the most frequent questions we're asked at Zingin.com is which search tool is the best. It would be great if there was one search engine which was capable of finding anything you want on the internet but, unfortunately, there is no one-stop solution. Sorry.

Having said that, if you want to quickly search the whole of the web, a quick look at our run-down of the leading international and UK search tools should point you in the right direction.

Don't forget, though, the point of this book is to point you towards the best sites for different types of searches, rather than just listing all of them and leaving the rest to you, so we're sorry if your favourite tool isn't listed. If you want to find out more about the ones we've chosen not to mention, it's well worth visiting Search Engine Watch (www.searchenginewatch.com).

## General global searches

So you want to search the whole web for a specific piece of information and you don't know where to start? If you don't mind getting results from around the world (especially the USA) then our recommended global search sites allow you to search literally billions of web pages without even breaking sweat.

## ■ The best of the best

### Google www.google.com

If we were stranded on a desert island and could choose only one search engine, then this would be it. Although Google is a relative newcomer compared with some of the old favourites, its highly intelligent search method has taken it straight to the top of the tree for both ease of use and quality of results.

Unlike other sites which simply match keywords and hazard a guess at what you're looking for, Google ranks

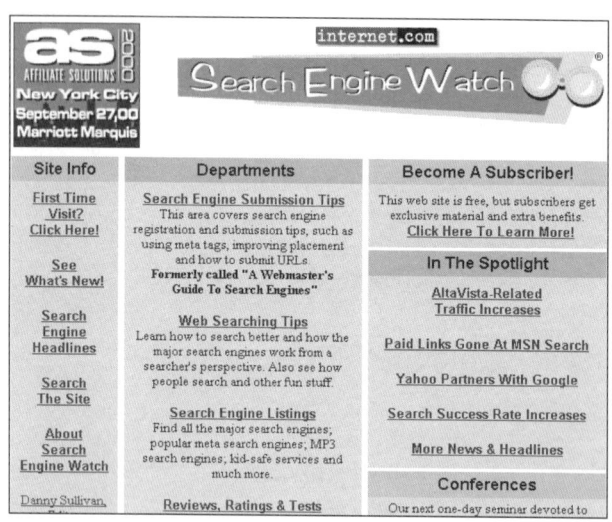

pages by popularity (how many other sites link to them) so you will always get the best sites first – in theory at least. In terms of coverage, although it can't claim to know everything, this search monster is capable of searching over one billion individual web pages (1,060,000,000 at the time of writing) so you're bound to find something of interest and, if you don't, there are links to the other main search engines at the bottom of each result page.

So what's the catch? Good question, it's a bit difficult to find one – it lists more sites than the rest, the results are great, the design is uncluttered and you can even do multilingual searches. If we had to find a fault then it would be the fact that Google allows companies to buy search keywords – so, for example, if you search for *spanners* you will always get a link to their site above all of the 'proper' results. Fortunately it's very simple to ignore the sponsored link

and, after all, most of the other search sites play the same game anyway.

Good for: Searching the whole web in a hurry.

Useful tip: If you want to find UK-specific sites on Google, simply type *UK* (or *.co.uk*) after your keywords.

## ■ The rest of the best

### Yahoo! www.yahoo.com

Yahoo! was one of the first sites to try to catalogue the internet and, until Google came along, it would have been our recommendation for the best place to start a web search. Although it offers a plethora of different features including email, chat, news, weather and finance, Yahoo!'s main attraction is its huge directory of sites which has been compiled by a team of human web surfers and is sorted into thousands of individual categories and sub-categories to make them easier to browse.

Because real human beings build its directory, you'd expect something pretty special – just imagine a directory without any broken links or poor-quality sites! Unfortunately, due to the massive number of new sites coming on to the web and old ones disappearing, Yahoo!'s surfers are unable to keep up and, as a result, the directory is full of broken links and some very strong adult content.

All is not lost, however, as Yahoo! will also automatically use your keywords to search the entire web for matching sites – using technology from none other than Google. If Yahoo! can search all of Google's database plus its own directory then why isn't it our best of the best? Basically, while Yahoo! can produce some excellent results, it's nowhere near as user-friendly as Google, and as the results are divided up into categories, websites and web pages, it can be a real chore to find what you need.

Having said that, if you try Google and don't find anything suitable (and you don't mind wading through broken links) then Yahoo! is an old favourite that's still well worth trying.

Good for: Searching a huge number of sites from one place.

Useful tip: For localised searching, try one of Yahoo!'s regional sites including Yahoo! UK and Ireland (**www. yahoo.co.uk**), Yahoo! Deutschland (**www.yahoo.de**) and Yahoo! France (**www.yahoo.fr**).

## AltaVista  www.altavista.com

Gimmick lovers rejoice! AltaVista has more toys – sorry, features – than you can shake a virtual stick at but, unlike some of its competitors, still manages to remain pretty easy to use. If you just want to perform a general search then simply type in your keywords and click the search button, but if you're hunting for something specific you'll love the additional features on offer. As well as the main search, there's an advanced option which gives you more control over your keywords and a range of media searches so you can track down freely available music, video and images with ease.

If you're new to the world of searching and want some extra advice, AltaVista provides a useful 'cheat sheet' to get you started and there are more tips displayed beneath the search box itself. One of the particularly nice features offered by AltaVista is the family filter, which prevents children finding unsuitable material – simply click the link next to the main search box and follow the instructions from here – but remember, no filter is 100% guaranteed to block adult content and there's nothing to stop kids surfing over to an alternative site like Yahoo!.

Good for: Family-safe, feature-packed searching.

Useful tip: For no-frills searching of their directory, check out AltaVista's Raging (**www.raging.com**).

## Hotbot **www.hotbot.com**

While Hotbot's database may not be as large as the likes of AltaVista (**www.altavista.com**) or Northern Light (**www.northernlight.com**), it's certainly the easiest site to use for complex searches. Using a very straightforward set of tick-boxes and drop-down menus you can tell the search engine to look for exact phrases, certain keywords, links to a particular page, people's names and much more – you can even ask for only pages which contain music or video.

Directory fans (you know who you are) may also enjoy browsing the database by category (Arts & Entertainment, Reference, etc.) but, if you do prefer drilling down through categories and sub-categories, you are probably better off with Yahoo!.

Good for: Complex searches, tracking down internet music and video.

Useful tip: The beauty of Hotbot is its search options, but if you prefer browsing by category, look elsewhere.

## Northern Light **www.northernlight.com**

If you've tried the top four and are still drawing a blank then it's time to try Northern Light. Who? Although it isn't as well known as the likes of Yahoo!, mainly because it doesn't spend billions on advertising, Northern Light is capable of searching a massive number of pages and usually returns some excellent results. Admittedly, the layout of the site leaves a lot to be desired and the bizarre system of sorting results into little folders may put you off initially (you can just ignore them!), but these aren't major problems and certainly shouldn't stop you from trying it out.

Good for: Finding sites that the others have missed out.

Useful tip: The folder system can be safely ignored but is very useful when you get the hang of things.

## ◼ The best of the rest

### Euroseek www.euroseek.com

Just when you were beginning to think that, on the web at least, the word 'international' could be substituted for 'American', along comes a dedicated European search tool. Or at least, that's what it claims. In reality, as with all of the other search engines, the vast majority of results we found were indeed American. Doh!

Perhaps this is due to the fact that the USA still has more websites than any other country, but you'd nevertheless expect this type of search tool to bring the European ones to the top of the list, wouldn't you? That criticism aside, Euroseek does allow you to search in any one of over forty languages and the results produced are usually pretty accurate, so if you're looking for foreign language material, this could well come up trumps.

### Excite www.excite.com

Although Excite is an extremely powerful search tool, its global search site produces a large number of American results. Its UK version (www.excite.co.uk), however, is excellent and full details can be found in the General UK Searches section.

# General UK searches

The internet is sometimes described as being the 51st state of the USA. While the Americans don't own the web, they certainly dominate it – as you'll have discovered if you've tried our recommended global search tools. So what if you want to restrict your search to local sites, or at least would like to find a fair mix from both sides of the Atlantic? Fortunately there are plenty of UK-specific directories and search engines which are more than happy to help. As well as the British-based sites such as UK Plus (www.ukplus.co.uk) and 250000 (www.250000.co.uk), most of the global search giants have created UK versions, with varying degrees of success. As a general rule, if you are looking for local content (UK news, sports results, etc.) then a site like UK Plus is the place to go; for more balanced results, head for Yahoo! UK (www.yahoo.co.uk) or Excite UK (www.excite.co.uk).

## ■ *The best of the best*

### UK Plus  www.ukplus.co.uk

More than just a web directory, UK Plus offers news, features and dedicated sections for Scotland, Ireland and Wales. When it comes to searching (or browsing) for UK sites, the directory produces some excellent results although, naturally, you won't find anything like the number you'd get on the international sites. The results are all family-friendly so it's fine for the kids but, having said that, as with AltaVista's family filter, you'll want to keep an eye on younger surfers because there's also an option to surf the whole of the internet with only a simple warning message standing between them and the big bad web. All in all, if you want to fight against the American domination of the internet, this is a good place to start – it's quick, the results are good and it's British, dammit!

Good for: UK-specific searches. This is one site that definitely knows the difference between Birmingham, England and Birmingham, Alabama.

Useful tip: If the search feature produces no results, try browsing the directory by category to find something similar.

■ *The rest of the best*

### Excite UK  www.excite.co.uk

While many of the American search engines are happy to stick *.co.uk* at the end of their name and claim to have produced a UK version, Excite is really making an effort to produce something different. Yes, you'll still find a whole load of US information, but there are also plenty of British sites and the balance is about right if you choose the right keywords.

Actually, calling Excite a search engine is like calling Disneyland a fairground – even if you don't want to use the search features you'll have hours of fun with news, free e-mail, shopping, chat, sport, weather and pretty much everything else you'd expect from one of the world's leading web portals.

Good for: UK searches, with a few international sites thrown in for good measure. The additional features are worth checking out, too.

Useful tip: Some of the features are shared between the UK and US versions, so don't be surprised if you find yourself chatting to someone in New York.

### 250000  www.250000.co.uk

250000 is so called because it is offering a quarter of a million free shares to users of its impressive UK search service. Compared with the likes of Excite and UK Plus, only a fairly small number of sites are listed, but they're all UK-based and the majority are of excellent quality.

The real attraction of the directory is the fact that it's sorted by region, so you can look for sites based in your neck of the woods, whether you live in Aberdeen or

Wrexham – although, as you'd expect, the big cities have more listings than some of the smaller towns. If you're looking for information for the whole of the UK (and beyond) then you'd be much better with the likes of UK Plus or Excite, but if you need to know more about local businesses and tourist attractions then this is a great starting point.

Good for: Searching for local information and businesses.

Useful tip: If you do want to search the whole of the UK on 250000, try using the search box rather than browsing through the directories.

## Search Engine.com  **www.searchengine.com**

Formerly SearchUK, Search Engine.com is like UK Plus but without the news and features. Like UK Plus, you'll find plenty of UK-specific results using either a standard search box or by browsing categories which include Business, Careers & Employment, Computers & Internet, Education, Entertainment, Environment, Health, Kids, Leisure and Money. Search Engine.com is slowly rolling out across Europe and at the time of writing there was a German version, with more promised – so keep checking back.

Good for: No-frills UK searching.

Useful tip: For European language searches, keep an eye on Search Engine.com's expansion plans.

## Ask Jeeves  **www.ask.co.uk**

Web searching with a friendly face is the name of the game here. Ask Jeeves was one of the first search engines to allow complete sentences (*where can I find Kendal mint cake*) rather than just keywords, and, as these types of sites go, it's pretty good at its job. The thing to remember about natural language search engines is that they still look for keywords to work out what you're looking for – if you ask Jeeves to find *the best UK search engine* it will come back with information about search tools but it will also suggest sites about the UK in general as well as those which contain the word 'best'. Having said that, the main advantage of using Ask Jeeves rather than one of the alternatives is the user-friendly way the search results are displayed. Rather than dropping you straight into a list of potential matches, Jeeves suggests possible questions that it (he?) knows the answer to, allowing you to choose the one which most closely matches your query – too much hassle for seasoned surfers, but great for anyone new to the web.

The design looks great, but we can't help feeling that the English Butler character must work better for American visitors (**www.ask.com**) than over here. And as for phrases like 'may one have your feedback?' – oh dear.

Good for: Natural language searching for beginners.

Useful tip: Try to put as many keywords as possible into your question to produce the best results.

## AltaVista UK  www.altavista.co.uk

Like Excite, AltaVista is making a real effort to appeal to UK users both with the quality of its content (news, weather, polls, etc.) and also a fair number of .co.uk addresses in the search results. If you're familiar with the American version of AltaVista then you'll be pleased to find the same features on the UK site, including the ability to search for different media types and the family filter to keep the youngsters safe. Splendid.

Good for: Searching for specific media types (music, video, graphics).

Useful tip: If you do find too many American results, simply type *UK* after your keywords.

## Mirago  www.mirago.co.uk

So many words, so little page space. Mirago seems determined to pack as much text on its front page as humanly possible and, as a result, loses some points in the usability stakes. Fortunately, there's also plenty to see and do on Mirago, with news, TV listings, tutorials and, of course, a search engine which was one of the first in the UK to allow you to filter adult material. The results themselves are pretty impressive and, in case you don't find what you want, the site even suggests searches which you might want to try. Nice touch.

Good for: Family-friendly searches and extra content.

Useful tip: Make sure you switch on the family filter option using the link at the top left-hand side of the page.

## ■ The best of the rest

## Infoseek  www.infoseek.co.uk

Seeking info? It may be a little light on features compared with the other search engines, but Infoseek looks slick and produces a decent number of UK results.

## Looksmart  www.looksmart.co.uk

A joint effort between the American search giant and British Telecom, Looksmart's directory produces some great UK results, but watch out for a thoroughly American search system.

### Lycos www.lycos.co.uk

Following a huge UK advertising campaign, Lycos is trying very hard to establish itself in the UK – and from the evidence here it looks like it's well on the way! Nice.

### Yahoo! www.yahoo.co.uk

Much as we'd like to praise Yahoo!'s dedication to providing relevant search results to non-US users, its UK version is pretty disappointing. There's plenty of British news, weather, finance and general info, but when it comes to searching, you're probably best looking elsewhere.

# metasearch tools

If you're searching for something particularly specialised then even the biggest search engines may not find anything suitable. If your favourite search tool doesn't do the job then it's time to try a metasearch site which will submit your keywords to all of the major search engines, returning the first few results from each to give you a quick overview of what's available. If you find something that looks interesting then you can jump straight to the relevant search engine or directory for the full list of results. While some people swear by the effectiveness of metasearching, others say that it doesn't give enough results to be useful. The best advice is to try out the following recommended tools and decide what you prefer.

Also, if you usually use the same computer every time you use the internet, it might be worth checking out Copernic (www.copernic.com) which runs on your PC and allows you to search all of the top search engines at once. It can be a little confusing to use at first, but it's a great time-saver.

the very best ways to search the internet

## ■ *The best of the best*

### MetaCrawler www.metacrawler.com

It's always pleasant to see an American site which takes UK surfers seriously, and MetaCrawler certainly seems to realise that there is life on this side of the Atlantic, allowing you to either search the whole web or stick to UK sites. Your keywords are sent to such search giants as Google, Infoseek and Excite and, if you feel like it, you can even restrict the results to MP3 files, images, newsgroups, auction items and directory categories. As you might expect, however, not every search engine is checked – especially the UK ones – so you'll probably still want to do a quick check on your

favourite site to make sure nothing is missed out. All in all, a superb starting point for quick web searches.

Good for: Getting a quick overview of UK and global search results.

Useful tip: MetaCrawler is owned by the Go2Net network and affiliated with several other companies, so don't be surprised if you click on a front page link and find yourself on a completely different site.

## ■ The best of the rest

### ixquick www.ixquick.com

Whether or not it's the world's most powerful metasearch engine, as it claims to be, ixquick is certainly up there with the best of them. All of the big search engines and directories are covered and you can even search for MP3 files, news and pictures, if you're into that sort of thing. The proof of the pudding, though, is in the eating, and ixquick's results won't disappoint you – you're told how many engines produced how many results so you'll know where to look in future. The extra features offered by MetaCrawler are noticeably absent, but when it comes to searching, it's clean, it works and it's extremely impressive.

Good for: Accurate, no-frills international searches.

Useful tip: Narrow down your results by selecting which sites will be searched using the tick-boxes at the top of each page.

### Dogpile www.dogpile.com

Another close contender for best of breed (excuse the pun), Dogpile differs from MetaCrawler in a number of ways.

Firstly, if a particular search site doesn't produce any results, Dogpile will tell you (e.g. 'Excite produced 0 results') so you at least know where *not* to try future searches on that subject – very useful if you're using a metasearch as a starting point for a number of searches. Secondly, the site only has a US version, so if you're after UK sites you'll need to look elsewhere. It's worth pointing out that both Dogpile and MetaCrawler are members of the Go2Net network, so don't be surprised if the results don't vary wildly. Having said that, it's still well worth trying both to ensure you're getting the best possible metasearch results.

Good for: Getting a third opinion, if the other metasearch sites fail.

Useful tip: When you've finished searching, check out some of Dogpile's other features.

5

# general expert guides

Expert guides are a form of directory in so far as they employ human beings to build up a list of relevant sites, arranged into different subject areas. However, unlike a standard directory, this type of site will usually employ experts in different fields to maintain each of the categories – ensuring not only that all of the relevant sites are listed but also offering useful advice to make using them easier.

The labour-intensive nature of running an expert guide is such that there are only a relatively small number of general ones, but there is no shortage of sites dedicated to specialist subjects – see Chapter 8 on Specialist Searches for some examples.

■ *The best of the best*

About **www.about.com**

The original expert guide site, About has been around for years and offers a massive amount of information on almost every conceivable subject. Each of the subjects (from Art to Zoology) is maintained by an expert guide who also provides articles and general advice as well as moderating discussion forums and generally helping out where needed. There's even a little picture of your guide in the top corner of each section, giving the site a very friendly feel. If you're looking for local information, there's a UK version of the site (**www.about.co.uk**) which is nowhere near as comprehensive as the main guide but is slowly gathering momentum – it's worth checking out, but until it gets more UK guides, there will continue to be plenty of American content. About isn't really suited to quick searches, but it's great if you want to find out as much as possible about a particular subject. There's a definite sense of community, with users swapping information in the forums and plenty of questions and answers to keep things flowing. Simply the best.

## ■ *The rest of the best*

### The Open Directory Project **www.dmoz.org**

Rather than attempting to keep track of the huge growth of the web on its own, Netscape launched the Open Directory Project, which relies on thousands of enthusiastic amateur volunteers to browse the web and add sites to the database. The idea is simple enough, but it works extremely well – with a higher standard of links than some of the automated sites, and brief descriptions of the sites to keep you on the right track.

Don't be surprised if you find the Open Directory being used on other sites – including Lycos, Hotbot and Google – Netscape has generously offered access to the database to anyone who wants it.

Good for: Browsing by category for popular information (music, news, etc.).

Useful tip: If you have expertise in a particular subject, why not become a directory editor?

### The Hitchhiker's Guide to the Galaxy **www.h2g2.com**

There can't be many sites which can claim to be an expert guide to the entire galaxy but, then again, there aren't many authors like Douglas Adams. The Hitchhiker's Guide is like a tourist information site for alien visitors and attempts to explain everything there is to know about earth and beyond from the sensible ('All about Brussels, Belgium') to the bizarre ('Train Station Psychosis'). A word of warning: if you plan to visit this huge site during your lunch break, don't expect to do any more work for the rest of the day. As addictive as it is brilliant.

Good for: Wasting hours and hours and hours.

Useful tip: Keep your tongue firmly in your cheek when visiting!

## All Experts  www.allexperts.com

Another American site, this time offering question-and-answer-style advice on a range of subjects from auto repairs to UFO sightings. Thousands of expert guides are standing by to take your questions so, whatever you've always been dying to ask, you'll find the answers here.

Good for: Getting free answers to life's questions.

Useful tip: If you don't get accepted as an Open Directory guide, this one's worth a try!

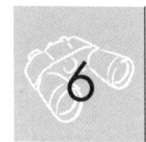

6

# young people's search resources

Of course the major search tools will produce plenty of results for younger surfers if you use the right keywords, but if you're looking for sites specifically aimed at the under-16s you'll want to check out one of the excellent family-friendly directories.

## ■ The best of the best

### Yahooligans! www.yahooligans.com

In case the name doesn't give it away, this is Yahoo!'s attempt at attracting future web addicts with fun, games and a huge directory of child-friendly sites. The design is suitably bright and over the top – although it might well give adults a headache – and the links are chunky enough to be used by even the youngest web surfers. The sites listed have all been reviewed by human search guides to ensure that no dodgy material slips through but, as there isn't a UK version yet, you might still want to give younger kids a hand when using it to prevent them getting utterly confused by the American spelling and talk of US national holidays. Also, as with any site, the fact that Yahooligans! is child-friendly doesn't stop more tech-savvy children simply typing in the address of a less suitable site, so it's still very important to supervise them at all times. Having said all that, if you want to get your family started on the web, this is a great way to do it.

## ■ The rest of the best

### Ask Jeeves for Kids  www.ajkids.com

Another tool which seems convinced that children love sites which look like they've been designed by three-year-olds (perhaps they do). Ask Jeeves for Kids allows children

to search using real questions rather than just keywords. The only minor problem with this way of doing things rather than having a browsable directory is that if younger users don't pick the right keywords then it can be very difficult to get the right results. Minor criticisms aside, Jeeves will probably appeal strongly to kids aged 5–10 who are old enough to know what the internet is about but need a bit of help (and a safe environment) to find stuff to do – and there's a great 'Jeeves I'm bored' option which will prove invaluable during school holidays.

## Surf Monkey  www.surfmonkey.com

More cluttered design (hooray!), this time from the bizarrely titled Surf Monkey – a portal which seems to be aimed at slightly older children than Ask Jeeves for Kids. There are plenty of features, including a guide to cool sites, fun and games, competitions, discussion forums and even the Surf Monkey club which offers email, chat, bulletin boards and a birthday wish list.

## Bonus  www.bonus.com

Bonus is packed full with the usual mix of child-safe surfing and assorted fun stuff, but the neat twist here is Netscooter, which causes the site to open in a new window, without an address bar or menu options. This means that unless kids know their way around Internet Explorer, they can't wander off to an unsuitable site. The features offered on Bonus are excellent, the layout is impressive and kids will no doubt love it – but parents might be a little concerned by the amount of advertising that their little ones are bombarded with on the site. When we visited there was an advertisement for a new movie with the message 'this is a great new movie, come check it out' to entice visitors to find out more. Oh, and the background music will drive you up the wall. Enjoy.

# businesses and services

There are probably two reasons why you would be searching for a business or service on the web. The first is to find the contact details for a local business (hotel, restaurant, cinema, locksmith), in which case you will want to use a *business directory* – the online equivalent of Yellow Pages – to find a list of relevant companies. The second type of search is to find an online business which will allow you to order a particular product or service over the web. This type of business can be found with the aid of a *shopping portal*, which allows you to search by product name, type, location and will even find the one which offers the best price.

## Business directories

Finding information about bird watching and nuclear disarmament is one thing, but what if you've got a leaking tap and need to find a plumber? Search engines and directories are great for finding web pages, but if the company you're looking for doesn't have a website then you're not going to have much luck – which is where business directories come in. This type of directory acts like an online version of the phone book, allowing you to search for a business or service by business type, name, location or services offered. Simply tell it you need a plumber in Poole or a wool shop in Woolwich and you'll be offered a list of possible matches complete with contact info and, if they have one, a link to their website. Simple really.

## ■ The best of the best

### Scoot www.scoot.co.uk

Scoot also exists as a telephone enquiry service, but it's on the web where it really excels. Using this superb resource couldn't be easier – simply type in the kind of company you are looking for and where you'd like it to be based, and Scoot will present you with a list of businesses and services, ranked according to how near to you they are. Once you've found the company you need, you can use the contact details provided to get in touch or, if you prefer, you can fax them, visit their site, call up a street map or even send them

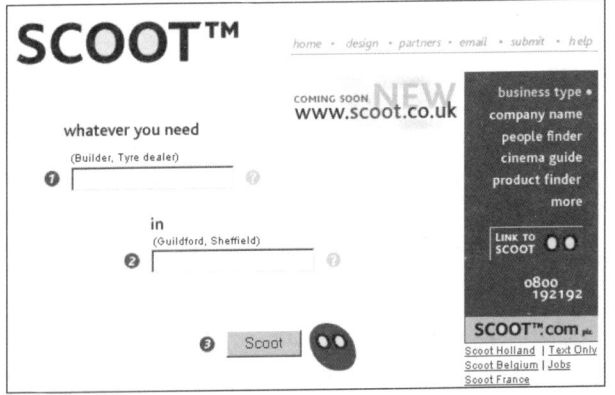

a text message – all completely free of charge. When you've finished looking for your nearest locksmith there are plenty of other features to check out, including cinema listings, product information, and a useful name and address finder. Superb.

## ■ The rest of the best

### Yell www.yell.co.uk

As you'd expect, Yellow Pages has been quick to establish itself on the web to avoid losing business to young upstarts like Scoot. Yell, as it likes to be called online, offers the usual search options – by name, service or location – in a surprisingly bright setting. The database is just as comprehensive as you'd expect from good old Yellow Pages, and with cinema, property, shopping, travel and weather info there's more than enough to keep you busy.

### Ask Alex www.askalex.co.uk

If Scoot and Yell don't produce any decent results, there are two possibilities – either there are no horse whisperers in Leeds or you need to look elsewhere. Although you may not have heard of Ask Alex, if you've ever looked for a business on the web then the chances are you've used a version of it as it provides search results to Freeserve, Dun & Bradstreet, VirginBiz.net and even the Department of Trade and Industry. The layout leaves plenty to be desired, but there are over 1.8 million businesses listed so you should have no problems finding what you want. It's worth mentioning at this point that all of the top three sites allow companies to pay extra to be bumped up to the top of the search results, so it's a good idea to look a bit further down the list before you pick up the phone.

## ■ *The best of the rest*

### County Web  www.countyweb.co.uk

This site covers 2.1 million businesses, separated into regional portals, which is nifty enough on its own, but when you also consider the other services offered by County Web you can't fail to be impressed. News, sport, places of interest, local police, property, jobs, cars, events, leisure, horoscopes and much more are available both on its website and on your mobile phone via WAP – and the design is not too shoddy either.

### Fish4  www.fish4.co.uk

Fish4's business directory is only a very small part of a huge network of sites which includes a property finder, local new sites, jobs, cars and shopping. The directory is very similar in operation to Scoot in that you can search by name, location or type and you are also given a detailed map to help you get there. The difference here is that with all the extra features available, you'll probably have no need to leave the house anyway.

### Multimap  www.multimap.com

OK, so it's not a search site; but once you've found the shop, hotel, cinema or restaurant you're looking for, it helps to have a decent map if you're not sure where you're going. Multimap is much more than decent as it allows you to enter any UK postcode or street name and instantly see a detailed map of the area. It's tools like this that make the internet worthwhile.

### Tapaz www.tapaz.co.uk

Tapaz is very different from the other directories as it is mainly aimed at business users who want to find other businesses. Having said that, it does list the contact details of thousands of UK and global companies so, if you are having trouble finding the one you want, it's well worth a quick browse here.

### Thom Web www.thomweb.co.uk

The official Thomson Directory site doesn't seem to have its act quite as together as Yell and Scoot. Yes, all of the directory search features are there, and if you don't find what you're looking for elsewhere then it's worth a try – but the design is a little uninspiring and most of the extra features (web and people searches, etc.) are actually offered by partners rather than Thom Web, so you may as well just use your favourite search engine or portal.

## Shopping portals

The number of online shops is increasing at an incredible rate and it's almost impossible to keep track of who's selling what.

Unless you know exactly which shop you want to buy from, it's a good idea to check out your options on one of the larger shop directories before you start spending. Different directories offer different sets of features, but the basic concept is the same: you type in what you want to buy and the directory gives you a list of traders which fit the bill. If you're buying on a budget, many of the directories will allow you to compare prices between hundreds of shops. You could argue that price comparison sites take the fun out of bargain hunting, but at least you can be sure you're getting the best deal without spending hours browsing. For the full run-down on internet shopping, pick up a copy of Zingin's *The very best shopping websites* in this series.

## ■ The best of the best

### Kelkoo www.kelkoo.com

Another site which proves that the best internet companies are the ones with the silly names (Google? Yahoo!?). Kelkoo is a truly global shop comparison site and, although some countries are better represented than others, over 25,000 merchants from around the world are listed. If you've got plenty of time on your hands you can browse the entire directory yourself, but it's much quicker to use the automated comparison system to sniff out the best price on books, music, films, games, computers, wine, electronics, toys, flights and a whole range of other stuff. Before you spend any money on the internet, make sure you shop around with this invaluable resource.

## ■ The rest of the best

### 2020 Shops www.2020shops.com

While Kelkoo is the online shopper's most powerful weapon, 2020 Shops is like a well-informed best mate. Other sites are busy developing automated shopping robots and search tools, but this directory is trying to give internet shopping a friendly face. What really makes 2020 Shops stand out from the crowd is not its huge range of features (there's a definite lack of gimmicks) but rather the quality of the site reviews, which have been written by professional journalists and are refreshingly honest and to the point. Whether you're buying a lamp or a lawnmower, a quick visit to this excellent site will get you on the right track in no time.

## Value Mad  www.valuemad.co.uk

The internet does strange things to companies. ASDA stores may promote their old-fashioned values and cheap 'n' cheerful shopping experience, but their Value Mad site is

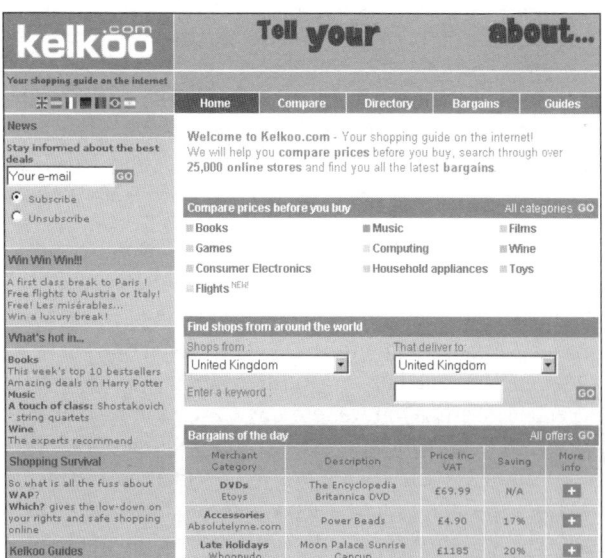

beyond funky. Split into three sections, the site allows you to get advice, find a shop and track down the latest hot deals, all with the aid of some colourful cartoon 'bots'. The number of retailers searched doesn't seem to be as thorough as Kelkoo and the information about each shop is certainly not up to the standard of 2020Shops, but if you are new to internet shopping and want that little bit of extra help, Value Mad should certainly be your first stop.

## Shopsmart  www.shopsmart.com

If you judge a shopping directory on the size of its popularity you'd find it hard to beat Shopsmart, which is one of the busiest in the business. At the time of writing there are over 2000 shops listed, with more being added every day, making it one of the most complete sites of its type in the UK. As one of the first UK sites to offer price comparison technology, it's had plenty of time to get it right, so it's a piece of cake to find the best deal on books, DVDs, games, music and video. The only downside to Shopsmart's popularity is that it lacks the friendliness that makes sites like 2020 Shops so usable but, if you're into cold hard facts, it's hard to criticise.

## Ybag  www.ybag.com

Taking a different approach to price comparison, Ybag makes the suppliers do the hard work so you don't have to. Once you've signed up for your free 'Ybag' you simply type in details of what you want to buy ('I want to buy a fridge for under £500') and they'll send your request out to their network of suppliers via anonymous email. If any of the suppliers think they have what you're looking for then they can send information directly to your Ybag for you to pick up at your convenience. The great part is that because the system is completely anonymous, you won't get pestered by salesmen or junk mail – if a suitable quote arrives then you can get in touch with the seller; if not, there's no pressure. Well worth checking out if you're buying expensive items. If you're looking for business products and services you'll find something similar at Mondus (**www.mondus.co.uk**).

## Shops on the Net **www.shopsonthenet.com**

It may be just a directory of shops, but this beautifully assembled site contains enough online traders to make even the most hardened shopaholic admit defeat. Very similar in execution to 2020 Shops, the site rates each shop out of 10 and also provides a mini review and some essential information to point you in the right direction. Some of the reviews are a little basic but, when you see how many shops are listed, you'll soon forgive them.

## Buy **www.buy.co.uk**

Now *this* is a good idea. Buy's goal is to take the hassle out of finding the best deal on services like gas, electricity, water and mobile phones, and it seems to be succeeding admirably. After you've answered a few very straight-forward questions, you'll be given a list of suggested packages and tariffs from all of the major suppliers. If you like what you see (and you probably will), you can simply click the 'buy' button to order online. Using the service is completely free and the advice is unbiased and very well informed. Nice.

■ *The best of the rest*

### Hoojit www.hoojit.com

Hoojit may be the new kid on the shopping directory block, but if its innovative approach to price comparison is anything to go by, it's destined to get very big, very quickly. Until then, you're probably still better off beginning your search at Kelkoo or 2020Shops.

### My Taxi www.mytaxi.co.uk

Offering you 'more time to have fun', My Taxi combines a shopping directory with a range of well-written articles and features. Having said that, considering how long it's been around, the service could be better. Worth a look.

### No Bags www.nobags.com

No Bags is clearly going for the youth vote with this fresh and funky site. Everything's covered here, from auctions to videos, and the content is more than acceptable. The potential is here for something very impressive, but at the moment it can't compete with the larger shopping directories.

# specialist searches

So, we've covered general searches, but what if you're looking for something very specific? The internet is chock full
of specialist information, from educational resources to
property prices, from tourist information to classic literature. There is insufficient room in this book (or any book)
to list every single specialist reference tool on the web –
that's what search engines like About (**www.about.com**) are for
– but to get you started, here are a few of the most useful.

## Academic information

Before e-commerce took off and the internet became a gold
rush, academic information was the main reason for going
online. Even today there are a huge number of educational
resources offering something for everyone. Although for
very specific searches (e.g. clinical psychology or quantum
mechanics) you will probably find better results by using
one of the major search tools (try Google), if it's more general information you need, learning something new every
day just got a whole lot simpler. For more details about
online learning, pick up a copy of Zingin's *The very best
family websites* in this series. In the meantime ...

## ■ *The best of the best*

### BBC Education www.bbc.co.uk/education

The BBC has been involved with the web right from the start, and if its current megasite is anything to go by, it will be at the cutting edge for a long time to come, with education as one of the cornerstones. From pre-school to higher education, you'll find something for everyone, including plenty of blatant programme tie-ins – all in the best possible taste, of course – and there's a superb internet guide if you're still a little unsure about all this web malarkey.

## ■ *The rest of the best*

### Schools Net www.schoolsnet.com

If you're trying to choose the right school, college or university for yourself or your kids then Schools Net could well

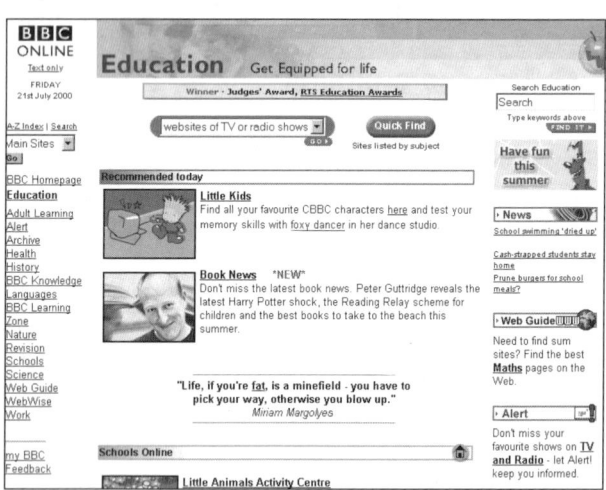

be the answer to your prayers. Along with an in-depth guide to 22,202 UK schools (count 'em) there's news, book reviews, revision tools, discussion forums and so much more. Very special indeed. For university information, visit the very nifty official site from UCAS (www.ucas.ac.uk).

## Search Gate  www.searchgate.co.uk

This massive directory boasts over 5000 academic, student and careers resources, all of which can be searched by category or with the aid of a handy search box. Although there's plenty of subject-related stuff here, the site is particularly strong on information for those in education (students and teachers) – so whether you're looking for advice on your GCSEs or the textbooks you need to complete your degree, this is a great place to start.

## ■ *The best of the rest*

## Top Marks  www.topmarks.co.uk

If Search Gate hasn't found you the site you need, Top Marks is the place to look for a second opinion. Over 1000 high-quality resources are listed along with descriptions, so you know exactly what to expect. It may not be the best education search tool, but it looks good and works well. Try it.

# Reference tools

On top of the internet's academic search resources, there are also plenty of reference tools suitable for everyday use, including dictionaries and encyclopaedias to answer all of life's questions.

# ■ The best of the best

### Britannica www.britannica.com

The online version of Britain's favourite encyclopaedia is certainly an impressive affair. Not only will you find the entire contents of the encyclopaedia, searchable by category and keyword, but there are also expert articles on a range of topical issues, a guide to the best of the web (sounds familiar!), international news stories and even a shop. It's worth noting that the site is actually based in the US so there are more than a few references to American culture and current affairs, but the reference material itself should appeal to everyone. Also, if you feel like spending a few quid in the Britannica shop then you'll need to visit Britannica UK (www.britannica.co.uk) which, at the time of writing, simply consists of a link to the UK shop and

another to the American site. All in all a superb reference tool with enough information to satisfy anyone's hunger for knowledge. Great stuff.

## ■ *The rest of the best*

### xrefer **www.xrefer.com**

'The web's reference engine' is a truly comprehensive affair, allowing you to instantly search a huge number of reference sources, from the *Bloomsbury Dictionary of Contemporary Slang* to the *Oxford Paperback Encyclopaedia* and the *Bloomsbury Guide to Human Thought*. The layout is as simple as you could wish, and the sheer volume of relevant results produced means that you may never need to pick up a dictionary, encyclopaedia or reference book again – oh, and it's British, too!

### Encarta **www.encarta.com**

Encarta started life as a CD-ROM encyclopaedia from the mighty Microsoft but has since evolved into something of a reference monster. Over 16,000 articles are available, representing less than half of the entire database – if you want the rest you'll have to pay – but there's also a dictionary, atlas and plenty of other Microsoft-sponsored content to make up for the shortfall. Like Britannica there's a bit of an American feel here, but if you don't mind replacing *colour* with *color* and *centre* with *center* you'll love it.

### The Virtual Reference Desk **www.refdesk.com**

If you don't fancy the idea of ploughing through loads of reference sites, then a quick visit to this simple but effective site, which allows you to search eight popular sources at once, could well be the answer. There's nothing particularly clever about the site and it won't find anything that a direct search wouldn't, but if you want answers and you don't have time to waste it's well worth a look.

## Dictionary www.dictionary.com

Simple but very effective, Dictionary will instantly check the spelling and definition of any word you throw at it. To be honest, that's about as far as most people will use the site but if you do stick around a bit longer, there are plenty of other bits, including tips on usage and style, discussion forums, foreign dictionaries and even a word of the day – just in case you can't think of anything to say. Of course, if you're not happy with the word of the day, you can substitute it for another one on the equally excellent Thesaurus (www.thesaurus.com).

## Travlang www.travlang.com

This no-frills site is a great first stop for learning the basics of a foreign language. Once you've chosen where you're travelling to, you are presented with a list of useful phrases which may not make you fluent but will certainly allow you to get by without resorting to mime. For more complex translations, check out Travlang's online dictionaries at dictionaries.travlang.com.

## Ask A Librarian www.earl.org.uk/ask

As if librarians weren't busy enough already, they've now generously given up their time to help internet users track down elusive pieces of information. Using the service is very simple, and very free: you simply type in your question, click the send button and within two working days you'll get an answer. So how does it work? When you ask your question, it is automatically routed to one of the participating UK libraries for a trained librarian to answer. The quality of responses, as you'd expect, is second to none – and when you consider that you don't even have to pay for the service, the deal becomes even sweeter. But the best bit is you can talk as loudly as you like while you type your question without the risk of anyone telling you to 'shhhh-hhh'.

■ *The best of the rest*

Encyclopedia.com **www.encyclopedia.com**
Inspired name, inspiring content. Not the best of the bunch, but a great way to find extra back-up information.

Funk and Wagnall's **www.funkandwagnalls.com**
America's favourite encyclopaedia hits the web.

## News and magazine articles

Some of the most useful information on the web comes from sites operated by newspapers and magazines. After all, most of them have been producing high-quality and informative content for years – and by publishing on the net, the articles and features live on long after yesterday's evening edition has been consigned to the recycle bin. Most of the papers and periodicals keep an archive of old material which you can search using keywords and, although some do charge for the privilege, most allow free, unrestricted browsing.

■ *The best of the best*

The Paperboy **www.thepaperboy.com**

If you don't know the web address of your favourite news-paper or just want to browse over 4000 newspapers from more than 150 countries, then The Paperboy delivers all the answers. You can search by title, city, country and language or, to restrict your search to British titles, there's even a UK version (**www.thepaperboy.com/uk**). Although you can't actually search for individual articles from the site, it will certainly point you towards places where you can. For UK local newspaper content, also check out Fish4 (**www.fish4.co.uk**).

## ■ The rest of the best

### BBC Online  www.bbc.co.uk

Before you say anything, we know that the BBC is not a magazine or newspaper. However, if you've ever visited its excellent website you'll know just how impressive its news and current affairs coverage is. Well-written articles are supported by video and audio clips, superb photography, external web links and much more – and it's all available in a huge searchable archive. First class.

### News Unlimited  www.newsunlimited.co.uk

You don't have to be a *Guardian* reader to appreciate this excellent joint effort between themselves and the *Observer*. Hundreds of articles are published online every day, and it's all stored in a searchable archive so you shouldn't have too much trouble finding something suitable. Well worth a look.

### The *Telegraph*  www.electronictelegraph.co.uk

The *Telegraph* was one of the first newspapers to realise the potential of the internet and its electronic edition should satisfy even the most news-hungry surfer. You'll need to register before you can read articles and search the archive, but it won't cost you anything and the quality and quantity of material is top-notch.

## ■ The best of the rest

### CNN  www.cnn.com

News on all things American.

The *Independent* **www.independent.co.uk**
Not quite up to the *Guardian*'s standard but a great effort nonetheless.

The *Mirror* **www.mirror.co.uk**
Tabloid journalism at its best, complete with a reasonably well-stocked archive.

MSNBC **www.msnbc.com**
NBC and Microsoft bring you the best US news and info.

The *Sun* **www.the-sun.co.uk**
The lighter side of the news? It's the *Sun* wot got it.

The *Times* **www.the-times.co.uk**
Feature-packed archive hidden behind a slightly strange layout.

## Health

The web has some excellent health resources, both in terms of actual medical advice and also support for those who are suffering from a particular illness or disease, but it's important to tread carefully. Unless you know who's behind a particular site it's probably not a good idea to believe everything you read, as anyone can put up a medical website without any proper qualifications. The best advice is to always consult your doctor before acting on any information from the web.

## ■ The best of the best

### Net Doctor  www.netdoctor.co.uk

Arguably the best health site on the internet, Net Doctor contains more information than you could shake a thermometer at, including an A to Z of diseases, advice on medicines, self tests, health news, discussion and support groups, and even an Ask the Doctor feature where a team of expert doctors, including TV's Dr Hilary Jones, will attempt to answer your medical questions. Whether you want to keep fit and healthy or are about to undergo an operation and want to know what's involved, Net Doctor manages to inform and educate without being patronising or difficult to understand. Completely indispensable.

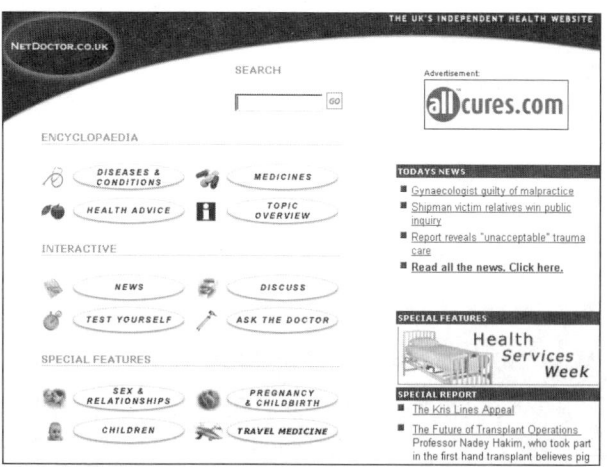

## ■ *The rest of the best*

### BBC Health www.bbc.co.uk/health

The BBC has done it again with this excellent health resource. Regardless of your ailment, you'll find information, support, advice and plenty of links to other online medical resources. As with the other BBC sites there are plenty of programme tie-ins, so expect to see the cast of *EastEnders* lecturing you on the importance of exercise and plenty of references to Holby City Hospital.

### Health in Focus www.healthinfocus.co.uk

Health in Focus claims to offer 'information, knowledge and choice' to UK patients, health workers and carers, and it seems to be doing what it promises. In addition to the searchable database of health information, there are advice guides, news summaries and plenty of other features to have you back on your feet in no time.

## ■ *The best of the rest*

### NHS Direct www.nhsdirect.nhs.uk
Excellent health resource designed to cut waiting times.

### Surgery Door www.surgerydoor.co.uk
Dr Mark Porter's guide to family health and fitness.

## Law and public information

The internet is all about empowering users by putting information in the hands of the people. Or at least it was before the people realised it was more fun to download music and pictures of film stars. Political, legal and consumer information is all freely available on the web both in the form of official government information and on thousands of enthusiastic amateur sites and, while you should always try to verify information found on the unofficial pages, you'll certainly find enough to ensure that you know your rights.

## ■ The best of the best

### Open Government www.open.gov.uk

The government may be confused about e-commerce and online taxation (bless 'em), but when it comes to providing official public information on the web they are doing an extremely good job. No matter what type of information you need you'll find a direct link to the relevant organisation, from local city councils and the monarchy to youth information and taxation advice. The search system works

more than adequately, but if you do fancy an alphabetical browse then it couldn't be easier. In a nutshell, if you want public information this is an absolutely essential first stop.

## ■ *The rest of the best*

### Find Law  www.findlaw.com

Despite being based in the USA, Find Law is a great place to search for legal information, regardless of where you live. The site itself bears an uncanny resemblance to Yahoo! both in layout and structure, with a search box backed up by a browsable directory. Bear in mind that you will get plenty of American information, which is obviously very little use in a British context, but if you dig deep enough, you'll almost certainly find what you need.

### Law Rights  www.lawrights.co.uk

If you do draw a blank at Find Law and don't mind paying a few quid for the privilege, you can get low-cost legal advice and documents on this excellent UK-focused site. Even if you'd rather not part with your hard-earned cash, there's still plenty of free information and a free lawyer referral service if you want to take things further.

## Money and property

Whether you're house-hunting or looking for up-to-date exchange rates, the internet is a great place to start if you know where to look. Luckily, knowing where to look is what this book's all about.

# ■ The best of the best

## Up My Street  www.upmystreet.co.uk

You can't fail to be impressed by the power and scope of this great tool which allows you to find out everything you could possibly need to know about a particular area (by postcode) and even compare one area with another. If you're planning on moving house and want to check the crime rates, house prices, school league tables and council performance before you make a final decision, then Up My Street is a godsend – and once you've moved, it'll even help you to find your local pizza delivery company or painter

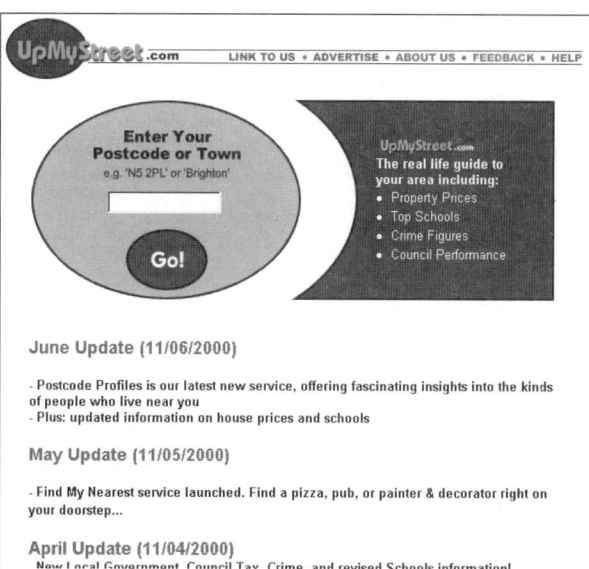

UpMyStreet.com    LINK TO US • ADVERTISE • ABOUT US • FEEDBACK • HELP

**Enter Your Postcode or Town**
e.g. 'N5 2PL' or 'Brighton'

Go!

UpMyStreet.com
**The real life guide to your area including:**
- Property Prices
- Top Schools
- Crime Figures
- Council Performance

**June Update (11/06/2000)**

- Postcode Profiles is our latest new service, offering fascinating insights into the kinds of people who live near you
- Plus: updated information on house prices and schools

**May Update (11/05/2000)**

- Find My Nearest service launched. Find a pizza, pub, or painter & decorator right on your doorstep...

**April Update (11/04/2000)**

New Local Government, Council Tax, Crime, and revised Schools information!

and decorator. This is what the web should be about – to use it is to love it.

## ■ The rest of the best

### Yahoo! Finance (UK and Ireland) uk.finance.yahoo.com

Yahoo! may not be the best web search tool any more, but when it comes to finance, it is still an essential site to book-mark. Up-to-the-minute exchange rates, share prices, insurance quotes, interest rates and coverage of the major financial news stories are complemented by links to the UK's top money and finance sites, making Yahoo! one of the best places on the web to find financial information.

### Screentrade www.screentrade.co.uk

If you want to find the best-value insurance on the web you can either waste hours trawling through the thousands of policies available or, alternatively, spend ten minutes letting Screentrade do the searching for you. Basically, you type in details of the type of cover you're looking for and the site will compare prices from the leading UK insurance compa-nies to find the best deal for you – even allowing you to sign up online using a credit or debit card. Simple, but very effective.

### House Web www.houseweb.co.uk

With over 150,000 properties for sale, House Web is a great place to start looking for a new home and, with a guide to online resources which help with the buying (and selling) process, you should have no problem finding what you're looking for. For a second opinion, try Asserta Home (www.assertahomes.com).

## Oanda  www.oanda.com

There's a huge amount of foreign exchange information to be found here. If your interest in the world's currencies goes beyond finding out how much French wine you can get for your pound you'll be spoilt for choice with news, up-to-the-minute rate information and even a currency trading game. Don't even bother with other exchange sites until you've been here.

# Employment

Looking for a job? We've all heard stories about how good the internet is for finding employment but, although there are some excellent positions posted online, finding them can be a huge job in itself. As you might expect, technology and media recruitment is extremely popular, but even if your dream job is slightly more down to earth, our recommended sites will give you a flying start.

## ■  The best of the best

### Monster  www.monster.co.uk

Thousands of jobs in a huge range of industries are available from the UK's largest employment site. Monster.com revolutionised online recruitment in the USA, and it has been instrumental in doing the same in the UK with a positions database searchable by job title, location, salary and industry. As if offering a huge number of jobs in some of the UK's leading companies wasn't enough, there's also plenty of help on offer, including CV tips and tricks, interview advice and everything else you need to get the job you deserve.

# ■ *The rest of the best*

### Gisajob www.gisajob.com

If you don't fancy the idea of trudging around the high street (or the web) visiting hundreds of recruitment companies then you'll love Gisajob, which allows you to search the job listings from over 5000 agencies – all under one roof.

### Top Jobs www.topjobs.co.uk

Another major player in the online recruitment world, Top Jobs lists positions in the UK and throughout Europe, allowing you to take advantage of the handy European freedom of movement thing. Très bon.

■ *The best of the rest*

Big Blue Dog  **www.bigbluedog.com**
Nice London-based employment site with a suitably stupid name.

Jobs Unlimited  **www.jobsunlimited.co.uk**
Position-packed employment site from the *Guardian* offering media, education and social services jobs aplenty.

Stepstone  **www.stepstone.com**
Still looking? Try this impressively clutter-free recruitment site for size.

# Leisure and travel

Relax – you work too hard! When it's time to take a break from the stresses of work, it's time to check out the web search tools designed to make life not just easier – but a whole lot more enjoyable.

■ *The best of the best*

Virgin Net  **www.virgin.net**
It would probably be quicker to list the leisure information which Virgin *doesn't* make it easier to find. Branson's quest for world domination continues with this massive resource which makes finding cinema listings, TV schedules, pubs, clubs, restaurants, theatre, days out, shops and even romance easier than it's ever been before. The layout of the site is busy but not cluttered, and, with search boxes aplenty, you'll find

it pretty straightforward to find what you're looking for. Obviously Sir Rick's companies are likely to get a bigger plug than their competitors, but it's a small price to pay for such an invaluable resource.

## ■ The rest of the best

### A2B Travel www.a2btravel.co.uk

If you're looking for travel-related information, no matter where, how or why you're going, don't leave home until you've checked out A2B Travel. A2B is the UK's largest travel information and booking portal. As it's designed by

publishing giant EMAP, you'd expect excellent design and content, but even by their normal standards this is something special. The layout may be a little cluttered for some tastes, but it only reinforces how much information is packed into the site. Whether you prefer to travel by plane or train (including Eurostar) you'll find timetables, online booking and everything else you might need. A2B has also put together a network of specialist sites which are designed to make your journey that little bit smoother. Check out A2B Airports (**www.a2bairports.com**), Escape Routes (**www.escaperoutes.net**) and A2B Europe (**www.a2beurope.com**) for starters.

## Digiguide  www.digiguide.co.uk

No more poring over a copy of the *TV Times* or squinting at Teletext to find out when your favourite programme's on. Digiguide is available both online and as a downloadable program that runs from Windows. Not only does it let you browse TV listings for the next couple of weeks but it's customised to your TV region and you can even ask it to alert you when a programme is about to start. If you have internet access at home, make sure you download the Digiguide program – it's free and you'll wonder how you ever lived without it. A real gem.

## Real Guide  www.realguide.real.com

Internet audio and video has taken off in a big way. Most of the large radio stations (and even some TV channels) around the world allow you to tune in online, using freely available software like the excellent RealPlayer (**www.real.com**). Once you've got the software you'll want something to listen to or watch, which is where the Real Guide comes in.

Simply type in what you're looking for, by country, subject or language, for a complete run-down of your listening and viewing options. Big-time internet radio fans will also want to check out About Internet Radio (internetradio.about.com) and Internet Radio List (www.internetradiolist.com).

### Internet Movie Database  www.imdb.com

Movie fans rejoice! If you want film information and trivia then there really is only one place to come. The IMDB started out as a small database of movies and actors but has since become the world's biggest and finest film information site. There are over 200,000 film and TV film titles to search, with info about the plot, the actors, the rating, the directors and pretty much everything else you could want to know. Love it.

### Games Domain  www.gamesdomain.co.uk

Stuck on level 4? Unstick yourself with this fun-packed gaming site. Cheats and hints are available across all formats including both console and PC titles – and there are plenty of up-to-date reviews to help you make the right choice. Game on.

### Ultimate Band List  www.ubl.com

Why waste hours looking for information about your favourite band when The Ultimate Band List will guide you straight to a whole world of official and unofficial shrines to your heroes. From Van Halen to Vanilla Ice, this huge directory features a huge number of artistes, covering the complete musical spectrum. There's also a well-stocked shop, plus some well-written content from UBL itself. Browsing the directory is hassle-free, with sites organised into amateur efforts created by fans, multimedia extravaganzas, official record company sites and the like, so you know what to expect before you click on a link. Rock on.

## Rough Guides  travel.roughguides.com

If you're searching for information about your next holiday destination, then Rough Guides has been kind enough to publish the entire contents of its books on the web, allowing you to get a feel for the place you are going to before you leave. Also, if all this travel information has fuelled your wanderlust, you can even book tickets and accommodation directly from the site. For the complete picture, make sure you also check out Lonely Planet (www.lonelyplanet.co.uk).

### AA Hotel and Restaurant Finder **www.theaa.co.uk**

Over 8000 UK hotels are listed and rated by the AA, allowing you to choose accommodation with confidence; and once you've got that sorted you can even find somewhere to eat. If nothing appeals, the RAC offers a similar service at **www.rac.co.uk**.

### Places to Stay **www.placestostay.com**

Finding a hotel just got a whole lot easier. Places to Stay brings together a huge variety of international hotels, with a very straightforward search system to find the one which best meets your requirements. This useful resource allows you to make an instant online booking and is an absolute godsend for business travellers.

### Funny **www.funny.co.uk**

The UK's finest comedy database allows you to search for some of the funniest sites on the web, all sorted into categories to make it easier to have a laugh.

### The Met Office **www.met-office.gov.uk**

A stylish site from those bright and breezy folk at the Met Office. Not satisfied with providing up-to-the-minute weather forecasts, they also give you access to satellite pictures, charts and climate information. Some official government sites can give you the impression that they've been thrown together in an afternoon, but it's obvious that the Met Office has gone out of its way to provide information in a clear yet comprehensive format. Outlook: bright.

## ■ *The best of the rest*

### Recipe Center **www.recipecenter.com**
American site with a huge searchable recipe database.

### Family Search **www.familysearch.org**
Track down your ancestors with one of the best worldwide
genealogy databases.

# 9

# searching for software

The internet is full of free software, much of which can be downloaded for just the price of a telephone call. Generally, unless you are willing to spend some money, you will only be able to get a trial version of the program you want, and it will stop working after a short period of time (usually 30 days). If you want to carry on using it after that you'll have to pay for it – but you'll often get a substantial discount on the normal retail price. To get your hands on the best of the freebies, try searching some of the following recommended download sites.

## ■ The best of the best

### Download.com **www.download.com**
CNET is already one of the internet's leading sources of techy news, information, reviews and gossip, and its download site is just as impressive as the rest of the network. Although there are thousands upon thousands of free downloads available, finding the one you want is a breeze – simply choose your format, type in a few keywords and you'll be presented with a list of possible files. Once you find the one you're after, it only takes a couple of clicks to

start downloading it to your computer. You'll be pleased to hear that it's not all serious stuff either, with a huge number of demos for the latest games, many of which haven't even been released in the US yet. Whether you're looking for a file converter or a racing simulator, there's no better place to start.

## ■ *The rest of the best*

### Tucows www.tucows.com

Tucows (Two Cows – you see?) is a slightly more funky version of Download.com, with a definite bovine influence. Not only can you search for freebies, shareware and demos

but there's also a software shop where you can download full licensed versions of popular software packages – no more chunky manuals or expensive boxes, and you won't have to wait for the postman to deliver. In our experience, you'll probably find Download.com quicker to use but if you can't find what you want there, this is a great place to look.

## Napster  www.napster.com

MP3: two letters and a number which are guaranteed to strike fear into the heart of any record producer. Basically, this audio format allows near-CD quality audio to be compressed into very small files (usually less than 3MB) – a breakthrough which has resulted in a wealth of music becoming available for download, causing concern in the music industry that pirate copies of copyrighted material will become widely available online. Napster is a free piece of software which effectively turns part of your hard drive into a storage bank of MP3 music while allowing you to search other Napster users' computers for tracks that you might be interested in. This community of music swapping has inevitably led to claims of rampant copyright infringement, with users converting their CD collection into MP3 format and making it freely available to the rest of the world. But, whatever your views on piracy, the software is a work of pure genius and it's a great way for new artists to get their music heard. If you want to be 100% sure that you only download legally available tracks then you'll also definitely want to check out MP3.com (www.mp3.com).

## Win Drivers  www.windrivers.com

If you've ever tried to install a new piece of hardware (printer, scanner, etc.) on to a computer without the proper driver then you need this site. Thousands upon thousands of drivers are available here for download, sorted by product type and manufacturer – and, although some of them are fairly large downloads, it won't cost you anything other than the price of a phone call.

## Icons Plus  www.iconsplus.com

The standard Windows icons aren't the most exciting in the world, and if you've been using computers for a while, you're probably starting to get bored with little pictures of disks and folders. Fortunately, in true *Changing Rooms* style, Icons Plus allows you to instantly transform your desktop into a chaotic mix of Star Wars characters, movie heroes, cartoon favourites and anything else that will fit into a little square. Good fun, but ever so slightly geeky.

## WinZip  www.winzip.com

Now that you've downloaded hundreds of games, printer drivers and R2-D2 icons, you need to uncompress them in order to install them on your computer. Your PC may well have come with a suitable unzipper, but if not you can get a very nifty one here.

# 10

# people searches

Finding web pages is one thing, but what about if you want to search the web for people? The web is full of tools which promise to make it easy to find phone numbers, postal addresses, email addresses and the rest – some of which are very effective but most of which are completely useless unless the person in question happens to live in America. UK users shouldn't give up hope though, as there is a growing number of sites which will help you find contact details for people in this country if you try hard enough. Even if you're not looking for anyone in particular, it can be a good idea to search for yourself, just to check what information others can find about you. If you do find information that you would prefer not to be freely available, it can be difficult to get yourself removed from the larger databases, but try emailing the webmaster of the site if you're worried.

## Email addresses

Almost every internet user has at least one email address. Unfortunately, unlike phone numbers, there is no central directory containing them so, if you need someone's address, the only guaranteed way of getting it is to ask them. Obviously, if you have no other contact details then you're going to have to try your luck on one of the following directory sites which rely mainly on people volunteering their information – so don't expect miracles.

To save trudging halfway around the web, E-mail Guide (www.emailguide.co.uk) allows you to search the most popular address finders from one page and, if you're looking for someone at university, your first stop should be the University of Reading's E-mail Finder (www.rdg.ac.uk/InfOff/dir.htm).

## ■ The best of the best

### Yahoo! People Search  people.yahoo.com

The only real difference between the various email search sites is the number of people in their database. Other than that, they all allow you to search by name, city and state (ahem) and offer complementary features such as address books, maps, phone number look-ups and everything else you need to become a fully fledged stalker. Due to the sheer number of people who use Yahoo! (many of them also using Yahoo!'s free email service) you can expect a fair number of results here – although, again, you're more likely to find 10,000 US citizens for every European. Worth a try though, eh?

## ■ The best of the rest

### Infospace UK  www.infospaceuk.com

Not the largest of databases, but this UK-specific site does at least know where Bedfordshire is. If Yahoo! lets you down then you might have more luck here.

### Bigfoot www.bigfoot.com

It's big and it has plenty of pictures of feet – but there's more to Bigfoot than just a stupid name. The site offers a people finder (naturally), a web search facility and free email – but it still assumes you'll want to search by state!

### Whowhere (Lycos) www.whowhere.com

Like Yahoo!, Lycos has millions of visitors passing through its virtual doors every day, so there's a good chance it knows how to get hold of a few of them. When you've tried – and quite possibly failed – to find the person you need, there are plenty of impressive features to get rid of some of the disappointment, including, somewhat bizarrely, an ancestor search.

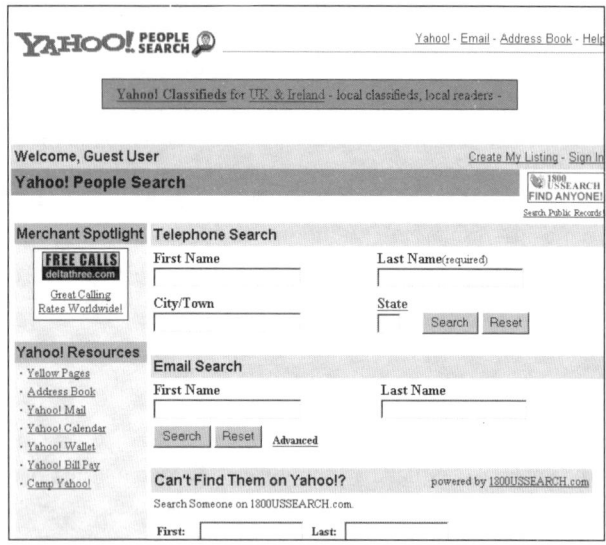

Internet Address Finder **www.iaf.net**

If you've got this far down the list, it's probably starting to look a bit desperate. Don't give up hope yet though, as there are over six and a half million people listed on the IAF. One of the nice features here is the fact that you can search by domain (e.g. *@zingin.com*) or organisation (e.g. *Zingin*), meaning that, in the case of business addresses, you might find one of the colleagues of the person you're looking for, who can point you in the right direction.

Switch Board **www.switchboard.com**

OK, now you can give up.

## Phone numbers and addresses

Unlike email addresses, finding UK phone numbers (even ex-directory ones) on the web is usually pretty straightfor-ward, and even addresses aren't too tricky. BT has thoughtfully put the entire phone book online, and sites like Scoot (**people.scoot.co.uk**) provide a very powerful means of finding addresses as well as phone numbers.

■ *The best of the best*

Scoot **www.scoot.co.uk**

Just when we thought we couldn't love Scoot any more, it only goes and launches a people-finding service with mil-lions of UK addresses and telephone numbers which makes it even more superb! Once you've registered your details on the database (giving one address in exchange for millions can't be too much of a struggle), you can search using a similar system to the Scoot business directory. Basically, you type in a surname and a region (e.g. *Jones, Chelsea*) and in seconds you're presented with a list of matching records, complete with telephone number and address – and you can even ask for a free map if you want to pop round and visit. A bit worrying, that last bit. It's huge, it works and it's free – well done, Scoot. Again.

## ■ The rest of the best

### BT Phonenet www.bt.co.uk/phonenetuk

In a nutshell, this is the entire BT phone book, searchable by name, address and region. Obviously you won't find any ex-directory details here, but if you're looking for a business, or a non-secretive person, then this easy-to-use, free site does everything it should with the minimum of frills and fuss.

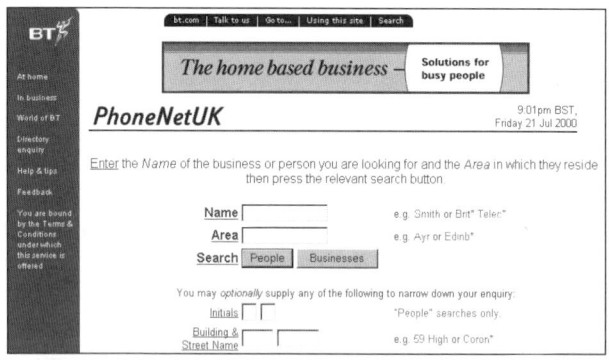

## 192.com  www.192.com

In theory 192 is better than BT Phonenet as it also contains some ex-directory information, but unfortunately it lets itself down in a couple of areas. First of all, unlike BT and Scoot, you have to pay extra to carry out unlimited searches and, although it doesn't cost a fortune, it still seems a bit unfair when the others manage to do it for nothing. Secondly, the last few times we've visited (and again at the time of writing) the site was unavailable due to the large number of people using it and, while this problem may well be fixed by now, it's just a little bit too much hassle. It's worth a look if the others draw a blank, though.

# discussion forums
# and mailing lists

Discussion forums and mailing lists make the internet more human. Instead of just surfing the web like a cyber nomad, you can exchange ideas and opinions on any subject under the sun, from aviation to zebra watching, with like-minded people from around the world. So how can you get involved? Read on ...

## Discussion groups

The most common type of discussion groups are known as Usenet newsgroups, although they have very little to do with news. There are over 60,000 groups within Usenet, and the most common way to gain access to them is with a piece of newsreader software which logs into your ISP's news server (if it has one), allowing you to find interesting groups, read ongoing discussions and post messages. Most ISPs offer access to much less than half of the total number of available groups, partly for reasons of space but also due to the amount of adult material found in some of the groups. Your ISP will be able to advise you whether it provides access to newsgroups, and if you're using Microsoft Outlook Express as your email program, you would also normally use it to access the groups.

If, for any reason, you can't access the newsgroup you want via your ISP, or you want even more choice, then the following resources will be right up your street.

## ■ The best of the best

### Deja News  www.deja.com

Deja.com's Usenet discussion service allows you to access and participate in thousands of newsgroups, whether or

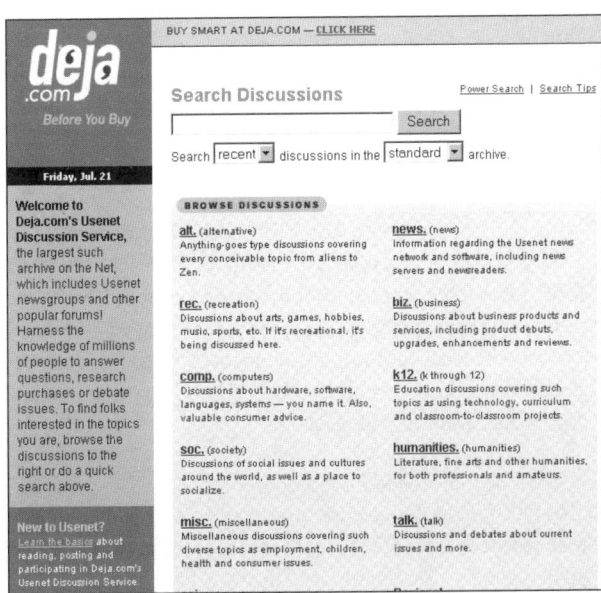

BUY SMART AT DEJA.COM — CLICK HERE

**deja.com**
Before You Buy

Friday, Jul. 21

**Search Discussions**                    Power Search | Search Tips

[          ] Search

Search recent ▼ discussions in the standard ▼ archive.

**Welcome to Deja.com's Usenet Discussion Service,** the largest such archive on the Net, which includes Usenet newsgroups and other popular forums! Harness the knowledge of millions of people to answer questions, research purchases or debate issues. To find folks interested in the topics you are, browse the discussions to the right or do a quick search above.

**New to Usenet?**
Learn the basics about reading, posting and participating in Deja.com's Usenet Discussion Service.

**BROWSE DISCUSSIONS**

**alt.** (alternative)
Anything-goes type discussions covering every conceivable topic from aliens to Zen.

**rec.** (recreation)
Discussions about arts, games, hobbies, music, sports, etc. If it's recreational, it's being discussed here.

**comp.** (computers)
Discussions about hardware, software, languages, systems — you name it. Also, valuable consumer advice.

**soc.** (society)
Discussions of social issues and cultures around the world, as well as a place to socialize.

**misc.** (miscellaneous)
Miscellaneous discussions covering such diverse topics as employment, children, health and consumer issues.

**news.** (news)
Information regarding the Usenet news network and software, including news servers and newsreaders.

**biz.** (business)
Discussions about business products and services, including product debuts, upgrades, enhancements and reviews.

**k12.** (k through 12)
Education discussions covering such topics as using technology, curriculum and classroom-to-classroom projects.

**humanities.** (humanities)
Literature, fine arts and other humanities, for both professionals and amateurs.

**talk.** (talk)
Discussions and debates about current issues and more.

not your ISP provides Usenet access. Using the service is very simple – it allows you to search for an interesting group either by topic or by name and then, once you've found a current thread (conversation), you can post a reply, ask questions and generally get stuck in. A word of warning, though: newsgroup enthusiasts are notoriously unforgiving of mistakes made by new users, so before you dive in, check out Deja's guide to the basics.

## ■ The best of the rest

### Forum One www.forumone.com

Not all discussion groups are part of Usenet. There are plenty of independent web-based forums which allow users to post messages on all manner of subjects. To find a forum that's your cup of tea, it's well worth checking out Forum One, which claims to list more than 300,000 of them!

### Supernews www.supernews.com

If you like your newsgroups to be free of junk mail then you're going to have to pay for the privilege. Supernews has been in the Usenet business for a long time and certainly offers a reliable way of getting connected but, unlike Deja News, it ain't free – although there's a free 30-day trial if you want to try before you buy. Another good (paid) option is Easy Usenet (www.easyusenet.com).

### Forté, Inc. www.forteinc.com

If your ISP gives you access to Usenet but you'd like a little more control over your posts than Outlook Express allows, you'll want to download a dedicated news reader – and there's none better than Free Agent (free) or Agent (not free) from Forté.

Liszts Usenet Directory **www.liszts.com/news**
So you've got access to Usenet and want to know what's available? You'll find a complete run-down here. Simple as that really.

## Mailing lists

Mailing lists, or email groups, work in one of two ways. The first type is a one-way mailing list where someone (usually the team behind a website) produces a kind of e-mail newsletter, filled with news, information and content dealing with a particular subject. Examples of this include Free Pint (**www.freepint.co.uk**), an email newsletter for business internet users, and our very own Zing-in Box (**www.zingin.com**), which is a guide to the best new sites on the web. To sign up to a one-way mailing list newsletter you simply visit the relevant site, type in your email address and you're away! The other type, which has increased in popularity over the past couple of years, is a two-way mailing list. Basically, once you've signed up to the list any message you post to the group is automatically emailed to everyone else on the list who can then reply to you in the same way. Most of the large sites have their own one-way mailing list so you shouldn't have too much trouble finding something suitable, but if you're looking for a two-way group, or want to start your own, visit Egroups (**www.egroups.com**) for everything you need.

## ■ *The best of the best*

### Liszts www.liszts.com

If you want to get involved with an email discussion list, you'll find more than 90,000 of them here. Either browse by category or do a quick search for something that interests you, send an email to the owner of the list asking to join, and in a few minutes you'll be up and running. Remember, before signing up to any list, it's a good idea to find out what their privacy policy is. Most list owners promise to keep your email address private, but it's worth double-checking to avoid receiving tons of junk mail. For more instantaneous discussion, Liszts also has a directory of chat servers which is well worth a look.

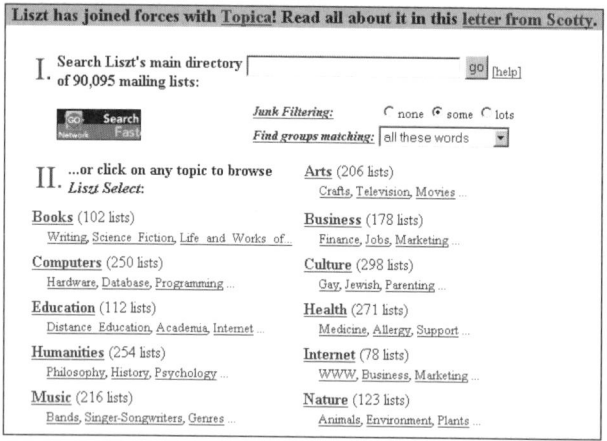

# ■ The rest of the best

## Egroups  www.egroups.com

Egroups provides the tools to allow anyone to set up their own email discussion group. If you fancy starting a group, it won't cost you a penny and will take only a few moments but, until you get the hang of things, you'll probably just want to check out the thousands of existing ones. An easy-to-use community-building resource, where everybody knows your name.

## Keep Ahead  www.keepahead.com

Keep Ahead is one of the UK's most prolific email news-letter publishers, with a wide range of free titles on subjects including news, health, trivia, food and drink, technology, sport and so many more. The content of the newsletters is always extremely well written and, as most are delivered first thing in the morning, they make a great start to your online day. Splendid.

## Free Pint  www.freepint.co.uk

Anyone who regularly searches the internet for business- or research-related sites has *got* to subscribe to Free Pint. Not only will you receive a monthly newsletter filled with search tips and tricks but you'll also get access to the Free Pint bar, a web-based forum to ask questions and exchange answers as well as a wealth of industry news, book reviews and a whole host of free stuff. Rude not to really.

## The Zing-in Box  www.zingin.com

A blatant plug. Sorry.

# 12

# information on the move (WAP)

The internet is great if you happen to be within easy reach of a computer. Although internet cafés have become extremely widespread, there are still times when it would be nice to be able to use the web on the move. The answer, of course, is Wireless Application Protocol or WAP, which allows you to view the internet (or at least a cut-down version of it) on your mobile phone. The number of WAP sites is still pretty limited and if you want the full-blown multi-media experience of the web then you're still going to have to rely on an internet café or laptop, but, if you can cope with no-frills browsing, the following recommended search and directory sites will lead you to the best of the mobile internet.

## WAP directories

Before you leave home, log on to the proper web and check out our recommended guides to the best UK and international WAP sites.

# ■ *The best of the best*

## Awooga www.awooga.com

It's fresh, it's funky and it's got a stupid name, but it's also one of the UK's most comprehensive guides to the wireless internet. In addition to a well-stocked directory, you'll find WAP-related news, downloads, books, advice and features to keep you up to date with this fast-moving technology.

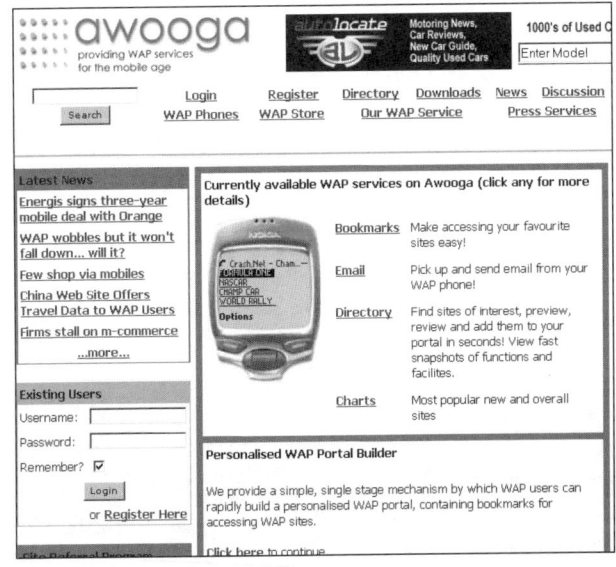

## ■ *The rest of the best*

### 2Thumbs Wap  www.2thumbswap.com

Another silly name, another great source of WAP links,
news, products and discussion forums. Both this and
Awooga should be essential bookmarks for any dedicated
mobile surfer.

### Yahoo! Mobile UK  uk.mobile.yahoo.com

It comes as no major surprise that Yahoo! has jumped on
the WAP bandwagon with this feature-packed but not
overly comprehensive directory. Well worth a look if Awooga
and 2Thumbs WAP draw a blank and, knowing Yahoo!, it
will grow quickly.

### WAPaw  www.wapaw.com

Another impressive WAP directory that seems to contain
quite a few sites missed by the others.

## Search tools accessible via WAP

Even if you're out and about, you can still search for the best
of the WAP world using our recommended mobile search
tools. Please note that the following sites are only accessible
from WAP-enabled phones.

## ■ *The best of the best*

### Google  wap.google.com

Already our search engine of choice, Google was the first
search engine to really 'get' WAP. Not only can you access its

entire database of sites (not just the WAP ones), but if you click on a link to a non-WAP link, Google will translate the page for viewing on your mobile, bringing the entire web to your mobile phone – another master-stroke.

## ■ The rest of the best

### Yahoo! wap.yahoo.co.uk

Yahoo! has transferred a large number of its portal services on to this impressive WAP site, but its use of the technology is still trailing behind Google – no change there, then. Having said that, the service is still pretty nifty, allowing you to check your email, read the news, browse the

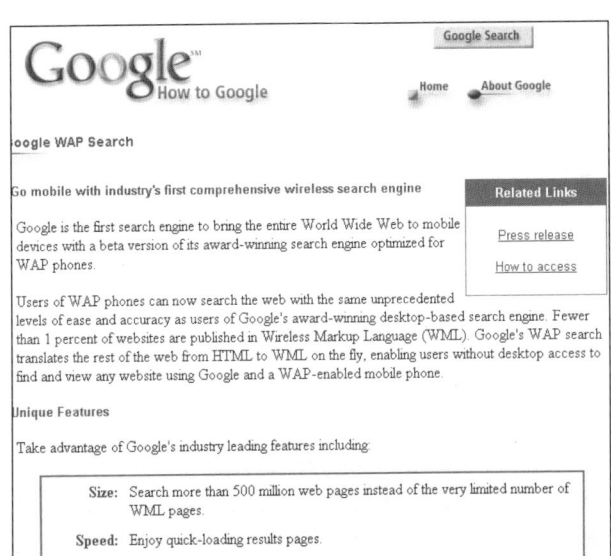

(limited) WAP directory and even send instant messages to your friends. Definitely one to watch.

### County Web  wap.countyweb.com

With County Web's mobile site you can access top-rate regional content from the comfort of your phone. Excellent.

## No particular place to go?

Surfing the web is fast replacing television as the boredom reliever of choice in houses across the world, and for good reason – there's loads to see and do and it's more interactive than staring at a flickering box in the corner of the room. The only difference is that TV doesn't require any effort, you can simply slump on the sofa, switch it on (not necessarily in that order) and aimlessly flick through the channels until you find something interesting. Or snooker.

On the web, unless you actively look for something you won't find it – which explains why at this very moment there are millions of people around the world staring blankly at their computer screens, typing random words into search engines to see if something interesting comes up. We've all done it.

So is there a way to stop this madness? Yup, simply look in on some of the internet's popular web guides which offer suggestions for cool sites of the day, weird sites of the day, popular sites of the week and a whole load of other starting points for your internet adventure.

### Cool Site of the Day  www.coolsiteoftheday.com

The site which started it all is still churning out a daily piece of online coolness to millions of web surfers around the world. The quality of sites varies wildly, but there's enough here to waste hours and hours and hours ...

## Hot 100  www.hot100.com

The week's 100 most visited websites. If they're good enough for everyone else ...

## The Netmag  www.thenetmag.co.uk

The UK's most popular internet magazine offers its recommendations for the best sites on the web.

## Web 100  www.web100.com

The 100 best sites in a wide variety of categories.

## *And finally*

Don't forget to check our daily pick of the best of the web at Zingin.com (**www.zingin.com**). You know you want to.

## Still looking?

Although we've tried to cover the most useful and interesting online search resources, we're not infallible (hard to believe, but true!).

If you can't find the information you're looking for then why not visit us on the web? The Zingin Guide (**www.zingin.com/guide**) contains all of the sites listed here plus an up-to-date directory of the best new resources for trawling the web.

Don't panic if you're still having no luck, just check our Search Guide (**www.zingin.com/guide/search**), where our team of human search experts will try their hardest to help you out – and it won't cost you a penny!

# quick reference guide

## General global searches

## General UK searches

# Shopping portals

# Academic information

# Reference tools

## News and magazine articles

## Health

# Law and public information

# Money and property

# Employment

# Leisure and travel

## Searching for software

## Email addresses

| | |
|---|---|
| WAPaw | www.wapaw.com 100 |
| Yahoo! Mobile UK | uk.mobile.yahoo.com 100 |

## Search tools accessible via WAP

| | |
|---|---|
| County Web | wap.countyweb.com 102 |
| Google | wap.google.com 100 |
| Yahoo! | wap.yahoo.co.uk 101 |

## No particular place to go?

| | |
|---|---|
| Cool Site of the Day | www.coolsiteoftheday.com 102 |
| Hot 100 | www.hot100.com 103 |
| The Netmag | www.thenetmag.co.uk 103 |
| Web 100 | www.web100.com 103 |

## Zingin links

| | |
|---|---|
| Feedback (Email) | feedback@zingin.com |
| Feedback (Form) | www.zingin.com/feedback.html |
| Home | www.zingin.com |
| Search Guide | www.zingin.com/guide/search |
| Suggest a Site | www.zingin.com/add.html |
| Search Engine List | www.zingin.com/guide/info/search |